BUYING AND SELLING WARTIME COLLECTABLES

An Enthusiast's Guide to Militaria

BUYING AND SELLING WARTIME COLLECTABLES

An Enthusiast's Guide to Militaria

Arthur Ward and Richard Ingram

THE CROWOOD PRESS

First published in 2007 by
The Crowood Press Ltd
Ramsbury, Marlborough
Wiltshire SN8 2HR

www.crowood.com

British Library Cataloguing-in-Publication Data
A catalogue record for this book is available from the British Library.

ISBN 978 1 86126 892 1

Photograph of Nick Hall on p.20 by Robert Davey.
All other photographs by Arthur Ward.

FRONTISPIECE: A member of the LDV in late summer 1940. The
soldier is wearing the army's early pattern denim battledress (all that
could be spared for such volunteer troops after the devastating loss of
almost all the BEF's clothing stocks in France). His ammunition is
carried in a cotton bandolier of American origin like his P17 rifle. A
civil respirator is still carried, however, as military pattern ones had yet
to be issued to such irregulars.

OPPOSITE: Second World War British button badge promoting the
benefits of milk.

739.7075

Designed and typeset by Focus Publishing, Sevenoaks, Kent
Printed and bound in Malaysia by The Alden Press

Contents

Acknowledgements

The authors thank the following individuals for their kind help in the production of this book. Those listed below either featured in or provided material used in the numerous photo shoots. They helped with research or provided fascinating recollections and anecdotes about the vibrant story of military collectables. Isabelle spent a lot of her free time keying her husband's often spidery text. Thank you. You all did your bit!

Richard Hunt, Roy Smith, Mike Llewellyn, 'Taff Gillingham, Ron Shipley, Herb Schmitz, David Wickens, Mick Sparkes, Nick Hall, Keith Homer, Mick Larkin, Neil Thomas, Isabelle Ingram, Nick Cordell, Paul Philips, Darren Steed, Fred Finel, Bob Whitaker, Keith ('Klaus') Major, Graham ('Otto') Lancaster, Julian Money, Paul ('Face') Glennon, Geoffrey Bradford, David Carson, Martin Brayley, Terry Voisey, Robert Steadman, Colin Wright, Neil Thomas, Christine Hunt, Jim Daly, Adrian ('Prof') Mathews, Dr Phil Heycok, Glen Mallen, Stephen Maltby, Andy Smerdon and Marie Taylor.

ABOVE: *Various British items from the Great War - an early RAF officer's khaki uniform (Pilot Officer rank); army officer's soft cap with adjustable cloth strap and tongued buckle; Duke of Lancaster's Own Yeomanry cap badge, military stop watch on a khaki lanyard, 'whistle referee type' on chain, a cast film prop copy of a .445 Webley revolver.*

OPPOSITE: *Cross-section of USAAF personnel both aircrew and ground crew in their 'Walking Out' (Class 'A') uniforms. Rear rank: Three NCO aircrew in Class 'A' jackets with wings. Note the ribbons for war service and bars denoting years of service ('hash marks'). A mixture of other rank's Service Caps and Garrison Caps are shown. The figure on the second left is a pilot holding the rank of Captain and wears the dark olive ('chocolate') blouson style 'Ike' jacket with officers' Service Cap. Front rank: The aircrew sergeant (far right) wears a personalised enlisted man's 'Ike' jacket. The figure (second left) wears an officers' dark olive service tunic with 'variant bullion' Lieutenants' rank bars on the epaulettes and an officer pattern peaked Service cap. The figures (far left and second right) wear both patterns of British made field jackets (the jacket second right being a variant of the Parsons Field jacket, referred to by collectors' as the M41). These jackets are made from the same material as British Second World War Battledress. The famous 'Ike' jacket was popularised by General Eisenhower who had a blouson style jacket, mimicking the British style. The figure (far left) wears the 2nd version of the British made blouson that mimics the official M44 Ike jacket.*

Introduction

Not all collectors readily conform to the stereotype of the spottily gauche reclusive, saddled with an obsessiveness bordering on mania. They come in a surprising variety of shapes and sizes and pursue their hobbies for differing reasons. Some of them are actually quite exciting. For example, Sarah Michelle Gellar of *Buffy the Vampire Slayer* fame, collects antique books, her favourite allegedly being a first edition of *Les Liaisons Dangereux* (she starred in *Cruel Intentions*, a contemporary adaptation of the famous French novel). She is also an enthusiastic collector of the works of the *Peter Pan* author, J.M. Barrie. Disco diva Donna Summer collects hand-blown glass; Michael Caine used to accumulate Galle and Lalique obsessively, but as he got older he decided that storing things in his attic was not sensible. Like her father Tony, Jamie Lee Curtis has a penchant for classic black and white prints, a favourite purchase being one of Dorothea Lange's seminal 'Migrant Mother' portrait from the time of the American depression. The Hollywood actor Cliff Robertson was handpicked by President Kennedy to play him in the 1963 epic *PT 109* and was an avid collector of vintage aircraft. The talk-show host Jay Leno collects old motorcycles and last, but by no means least, Queen Elizabeth II has probably the best stamp collection in the world.

The rock legend Neil Young has a passion for model train sets; a toy railway enthusiast in childhood, success as a singer/songwriter enabled him to rekindle his passions as an adult. Indeed, although most of his efforts were designed to benefit his son Ben, he built a huge layout and was able to purchase Lionel Trains, a favourite brand from his youth and the North American Hornby Trains. Closer to home, while playing the shadowy cold-war government assassin Callan, the British actor Edward Woodward revealed his character's passion for model soldiers. This and war gaming are Woodward's real-life hobbies and he co-hosted Tyne TV's seminal war game show *Battleground* along with the expert Peter Gilder. Militaria collectors can also count on celebrity brethren and one such pillar of the enthusiasts' community is the 1960s pop star Chris Farlowe. Playing in British skiffle groups since 1957, Farlowe signed with Decca in 1963. Although the industry recognized the quality of his vocals, it was not until 1966 when he and his band The Thunderbirds recorded a Jagger/Richards composition 'Out of Time' that he tasted success, hitting the top spot in the singles charts. He has been a badge collector since childhood and was able to put his new fame and wealth to good use, founding 'Call to Arms', an Islington-based Mecca for militaria buffs in the 1960s and the 1970s.

So, collecting, and particularly collecting militaria, is not as uncool as many might assume.

ABOVE: Two RAF aircrew in Second World War flying clothing. 'C'-type post-1941 flying helmets and 'G' (left) and 'H' (right) oxygen masks, Irvine flying jackets; 1941-pattern Mae West life-jackets. The airman on the left is wearing the observer-type parachute harness (this features a separate parachute pack clipped to the front as required for use).

LEFT: Reconstruction of a Royal Field Artillery (RFA) gunner at the trail of an 18-pounder field gun. A stiff service cap and tunic are worn, with cord breeches and puttees secured at the ankle, in keeping with the style adopted by the cavalry. This configuration reflected the predominant use of horse transport in field artillery. Over his left shoulder he wears a white braided lanyard, a regimental distinction of the artillery.

1 Military Collectables – an Evolving Hobby

THE BEGINNINGS

Put simply, apart from badge collecting, the modern trade in military collectables really took off with the expansion of army surplus stores following the Second World War. Although there was a significant trade in army surplus after the First World War, mass-production and the quantities of war materials that poured out of mills and factories in the 1940s created excesses which offered for its first serious, commercial exploitation (the thousands of unwanted biplanes purchased for a song by 1920s' barnstormers excepted).

In 1946 Europe was awash with the detritus of an Anglo-American army, which, anticipating massive casualties before the fall of the Third Reich, had been provisioned lavishly. This glut of militaria included most of the American forces' utility vehicles, as well as crate loads of British and American battledresses and webbing. The planners had assumed that the invasion of Europe would cause massive casualties and require large reinforcements after D-Day. Oversupply had been considered prudent. Fortunately, this profligacy was to the benefit of militaria enthusiasts and costumiers, and also helped to provide the armies of developing countries with kit and this, in its turn, became a source for collectors.

Traditionally, collectors of what we now term militaria were monarchs or wealthy aristocrats and until recently the British sovereign's collection of arms and armour was kept, mostly on display, at the Tower of London – it now resides in the Royal Armouries in Leeds – and the gentry and newly endowed nineteenth-century industrialists often displayed suits of armour or baronial shields and edged-weapons in their houses. The latter half of Queen Victoria's reign witnessed the flourishing of the art nouveau and the Arts and Crafts movement whose romanticism in the one case and praise for honest, unfussy workmanship in the other continued the fashion for medieval armour.

Before the World Wars of the twentieth century armies were relatively small. The Tower of London was literally the capital's reserve armoury, weapons to be broken out and distributed in times of crisis. Furthermore, before the advent of mass production uniforms were costly and took time to make. It was economically viable to reuse materials if possible and consequently obsolete or damaged items were unpicked and reworked; there were few surpluses then. So, aside from regimental collections of buff coats and the occasional Civil War cuirass, displays of muskets and swords, an elderly relative's proudly demonstrated souvenir from Omdurman or the Crown collection, there few enough items to encourage a trade in military collectables before the First World War, and what business there was happened by auction.

THE GREAT WAR AND AFTER

The 1914–18 conflict changed all this. The First World War was on such a scale that its effect on survivors and civilians alike was visceral. In Britain the creation of the Imperial War Museum was a cathartic act for those who wanted a monument to the sacrifice of those fighting in 'The War that will end wars'. It was a genuinely held belief that nothing of the kind would ever befall mankind again and the British government decided to keep examples of the uniforms and insignia of each combat arm involved.

The four years between 1914 and 1918 saw unprecedented technological advances in the development of weaponry. Man's malevolent genius created new war machines for use on land, sea and, for the first time, in the air. Examples of many of these were also preserved. Interestingly, the government of Belgium was pioneering in its efforts to preserve the uniforms and equipment of the belligerents, asking its citizens to provide examples of their wartime dress and equipment.

The exigencies of total war consumed *matériel* on an unimaginable scale. Raw materials were often in short supply. For example, old ammunition boots were recycled – churned up and used as fertilizer. Yet by the war's end there was an enormous surplus

Selection of British battledress cloth shoulder titles (embroidered and printed). Officially sanctioned for the entire British army in 1943, the differing colours drawn from the existing designations for branches of the service (that is, red for infantry, burgundy for the RAMC and red and yellow for armoured troops).

of uniforms and equipment. This could be stored or sold, and because the majority of the combatants' uniforms lacked the conspicuous colours of previous battlefield armies (French, colonial and the Central Powers services excepted), it could be put to civilian use. In the British army upon demobilization a soldier was expected to return his webbing, rifle and helmet, but went home with his uniform and greatcoat (which he was, in fact, expected to post back to his depot). Consequently, an enormous amount of surplus khaki existed. Added to this were a huge number of garments remaining in official storage, many of which were saleable.

The armies of the First World War were of an unprecedented size. They consumed uniforms and equipment with vigour – not least because so much was destroyed along with their wretched owners, often condemned to oblivion within the shell torn mud of no-man's land. But the coming of peace and the consequent demobilization created piles of unneeded gear. For once this surplus could be put to immediate civilian use as utility clothing and, in turn, established the first consumer-focused army surplus trade.

As a sideline, these dealers soon became a source of other, less practical items such as insignia, not just government issue but for unwanted battlefield souvenirs that Tommy Atkins brought home and sold on to raise a little money. Consequently, *Pickelhaubes*, broom-handle *Mausers* and a myriad Austro-Hungarian buttons and badges were deposited alongside the piles of unwanted jackets and trousers. Thus, side-by-side with the growth of the army surplus trade, with its occasional transactions in trench art and military equipment, the modern hobby of military badge collecting was born. Never before had British forces accommodated such a diversity of combat arms, regiments and services. The Great War spawned an exciting diversity of cap badges, especially given the proliferation of volunteer and 'pals' battalions.

The mood of the 1920s and the 1930s was mostly pacifist. Many had been traumatized by the violence and loss. Much of the appeasement prevalent at the time of the Munich Crisis nearly twenty years after the armistice was engendered by sin-cere politicians desperate to avoid the abyss of trench warfare accompanied by what Winston Churchill called 'perverted science' namely, the development of gas warfare and the new monoplane bombers. Even the famous manufacturer Britains switched from the production of lead soldiers to additional ranges of civilian and farming toy figures and accessories. Interestingly, Nazi Germany's *Elastolin* increased the production of its range of composite soldiers. People were sick and tired of war and wanted a respite from the bleak images associated with militarism. In sympathy with the general mood of the times and because the shocking memories of the war were still so firmly rooted in the collective memory, most people thought that to collect militaria was neither fashionable nor morally appropriate. People wanted to look forward not backwards.

THE SECOND WORLD WAR AND AFTER

The Second World War was seen from a different perspective. For the allies (also the victors, of course) it was a struggle for democracy against the excesses of fascism and totalitarianism and so when this war ended in 1945 it was considered fitting and patriotic to celebrate the military achievements of the allies.

The peace dividend brought a similar situation regarding surplus military stock. However, because fighting took place over a greater area than during 1914–18, unwanted allied equipments were deposited in vast quantities around the globe but most notably in Europe. Now established for more than twenty years, it was relatively straightforward for the existing military surplus businesses to deal with governments and purchase this redundant stock.

The cosmopolitan nature of wartime Britain was a further factor. Civilians, mainly the young, had been brought face to face with soldiers from many nations. This was an especial boost to badge collecting since servicemen from the USA, France, Poland, Czechoslovakia, Canada, Australia, South Africa and India, to name but some, were a ready source of insignia for enthusiastic schoolboy collectors.

Although the war had perhaps not left the aftershock of the Great War, combat veterans or civilians who had lived through

Three members of the Royal Sussex Regiment in early pattern Battle Dress manning an early pattern Vickers Gun. This is the most desirable Vickers machine gun because, being of the fluted jacket variety, it is most associated with the Great War. Later versions were smooth jacketed. Surviving deactivated weapons on the international collectors' market are mostly of Australian origin, this country being one of the last to hold on to its wartime stocks.

Selection of images of Second World War RN officers' pith helmet. The illustrations shown include the helmet accompanied by its Japanned-carrying box; the interior of this privately purchased helmet shows the manufacturer's details and chinstrap arrangement. In white finish to match the Navy's tropical 'whites', this helmet is identifiably RN and not colonial nor RM in origin by virtue of the blue band at the top of the folding 'Pugrie' headband. There is a rating's version of this helmet identifiable by being Ordnance marked (mass-produced). Similar helmets were worn by all three of the British armed forces; however by the Second World War they were effectively obsolete, this is evidenced by the fact that, although part of the regular issue for troops in hotter areas, they were frequently dumped on arrival in favour for the more practical bush hats or steel helmets once in theatre.

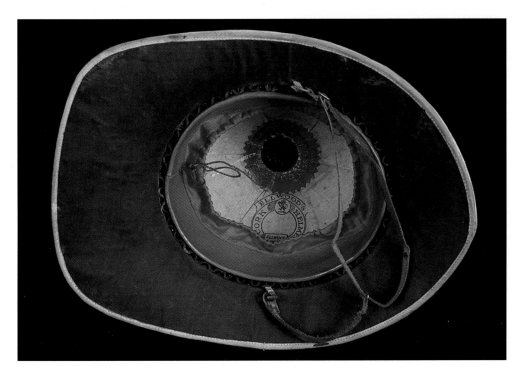

This example of a British Second World War civil defence Mk II helmet perfectly illustrates the conundrum these artefacts often present – knowing exactly what it is. Do the letters 'CS' stand for 'Casualty Station'? Diamond shapes were often used to signify a gas identification operative, but a source for this helmet shown has eluded the authors – any suggestions would be gratefully received!

the *Blitz*, for example, were still keen to forget much of the detail of six years of struggle and heartbreak, other than the solemn commemoration of fallen comrades or loved ones. On the whole, it has been the generations reaching maturity after 1945 which are keen to learn more about the struggles their relatives had endured; these really began the modern interest in military collectables. Founded on an infrastructure of established army-surplus dealers and supplemented by house clearances during the 1960s that unearthed treasures from the Great War, many businesses gradually transformed themselves into suppliers of military antiques and collectables. Interestingly, this was given an enormous boost by changes in popular taste. The years immediately following each of the two World Wars had been forward looking – art deco, the Bauhaus, Futurism, the Dior 'New Look', rock and roll – the old was unfashionable. However, in the 1960s the passing of the last of the 'Imperial generation' coincided with the adoption of much that had been familiar to them. The fashion in Victoriana was in harmony with the resurgence in Art Nouveau – most student flats displaying at least one Mucha print, swinging London embraced Victorian military style as in the Beatles' outfits in *Sergeant Pepper*, the pin-up David Hemmings in *The Charge of the Light Brigade* and Biba; red officer's jackets suddenly became popular and the Mods eagerly sought Korean War parkas.

As dealers sought out more nineteenth-century garments for the fashionista, uniform items such as insignia and equipment

British Second World War Mk II AFS helmet. Dating from early in the war, this is perhaps less typical being black rather than the more recognized grey.

such as helmets and shakos were made available to collectors and Hollywood inadvertently helped again, with films such as *Waterloo* providing an enormous popular boost to the subject. As mentioned earlier, the product of house clearances unearthed many of the military collectables traded today. By the early 1970s business in Third Reich militaria took off with many of the items handled being the result of an occupying soldier's successful theft, barter or embezzlement.

With Nazi symbols and insignia being proscribed in post-war Germany, an underground trade developed. The supply of authentic items had been limited by the not surprising desire of surrendering German soldiers not to be found with any runic symbols suggesting their possible involvement in war crimes. Nevertheless, many daggers and quite a few *Lugers* were 'requisitioned'; consequently, such items as did reach the market had financial value and were worth faking. In general, if something does not look right it is likely a fake. Indeed, the most common fakes are unfinished Nazi daggers – hoards of incomplete articles came to light in disused warehouses following the end of hostilities. The most common failings were the wrong hilt and blade.

Royal Air Force sergeant pilot of the Battle of Britain period. This photograph illustrates the 'D'-type mask and Mk IV goggles (worn in use). Over his other ranks' service Dress the pilot wears an Irvine 'parachute suit', a form of flight overall with a built-in Mae West bladder and an attachment point for a service parachute.

The final development in the field of military collectables, the acquisition of previously less desirable utilitarian items, such as webbing and field equipment, was encouraged by the activities of historic vehicle enthusiasts and 'living history' groups. The former required period uniforms, stores and equipment to ensure the authenticity of military vehicle rallies and the latter, the re-enactors, for use in educational outreach presentations or in special exhibitions or displays. Most of these items resided in huge warehouses, crammed with ex-government stocks. Warehouses have been the traditional wholesalers for war surplus material – they bought webbing, for instance, in bulk as it became officially discarded, with a change in pattern or use in the armed services' garb. Much of this bounty trickled down to army surplus stores at auction. This commerce included vehicles, radios and tools, alongside webbing and equipment containers such as packs and pouches. Many students in higher education during the 1970s used British army small packs or even Second World War respirator cases to transport their books and papers between lectures.

Second World War British naval rating in 'black top' rating's cap with plain wartime 'HMS' tally and wearing a sailor's 'top blue serge' (jumper) over a 'square-necked white front shirt' with 'blue jeans' separate collar, 'black silk' (scarf) and white duty lanyard. On his sleeve is a 'leading hands' red anchor rank badge – being embroidered in red cotton, this form of insignia was worn on working dress in comparison with the gold wire rank and branch badges won on best uniforms (a 'tiddly suit').

COMING TO THE PRESENT

By the mid 1970s, Second World War British and American military utility equipment had become elevated to the status of collectors' items. Collectors needed references to help them to identify authentic items and their enthusiastic demand for information encouraged the growth of publications such as Osprey's seminal *Men-at-Arms* series and the indispensable works of authors such Brian L. Davis and Martin Windrow.

As reference sources illustrated the variety of uniforms and insignia required to support 'total war', enthusiasts extended their area of interests beyond the gear of fighting soldiers. The service dress of home defence forces including the Home Guard, the ARP and the fire services were sought. Soon afterwards collectors realized that the women's services offered fascinating yields and within no time WAAF, WRNS, ATS and Women's Land Army gear became the targets for inquisitive fans. Fortunately, this enthusiasm has meant that a great many historical artefacts, once thought humdrum by academic historians but crucial in appreciating social history, have been preserved for posterity. However, it has also meant that there are not many gems still left to be unearthed. Collectors have virtually exhausted the surviving stocks of authentic gear.

Today there is a thriving industry for the manufacture of replica uniforms – the source of most garments worn by re-enactors and military vehicle enthusiasts. Many of these legitimate replicas, often manufactured in India, Pakistan or China, are of such a high standard that they find there way into the military collectables trade and are passed off as authentic. It is the rarity of even the most ordinary Second World War items that has forced many of the established militaria dealers to branch into costume hire which often requires the supply of a visually pleasing approximation of the original.

The absence of authentic battledress blouses and leather flying helmets from junk shops and car boot sales has encouraged enthusiasts to adopt some drastic, perhaps desperate, measures in their search for military relics. Consequently, there is now a big trade in the sale of battlefield relics unearthed from fields and hedgerows, invariably rusty and deformed, many of these items are unrecognizable and, frankly, of little investment value. Many question the activities of those who dig trenches among the last resting places of the fallen, disturbing them in the pursuit of personal gain. However, it must also be said that the activities of some enthusiasts have provided conclusive answers to the whereabouts of unidentified servicemen and the precise location of war-time engagements.

Curiously, enthusiasts now consider the militaria used in television shows such as *Band of Brothers* or in films such as *Saving Private Ryan* to be collectable – a case of life mirroring art. In fact, this recent development is not so strange and has occurred because now the traditional costume houses are no longer the first source of items for the production companies. Now it is easier for a company to purchase authentic items from collectors and dealers in original material or manufacturers of 'repro' equipment. As soon as a production 'wraps', these materials are unwanted but, in an effort to reduce production costs, some expense is recouped by selling them back to collectors. This is a new phenomenon. When the production of Richard Attenborough's *A Bridge Too Far* ended, all the uniforms seen on screen went straight back to the custody of the production costumier Bermans (later Berman's & Nathan's, and now Angels, a costume supplier dating back to 1840).

In the 1960s and the 1970s the established costume houses would never countenance any one asking to buy props. In fact and wrongly, the uninitiated assumed that the film studios held vast quantities of authentic costumes. While this was certainly true of the major studios such as MGM, 20th Century Fox and Columbia during the golden age of Hollywood, it should not be forgotten that the establishment of these studios in California was from scratch on largely green-field sites, unlike the European film companies which evolved from a long theatrical tradition, calling upon the services of long-established costumiers. Although British studios at Bray, Elstree and Shepperton could call upon some of in-house props, external professionals such as Angels and Southall's famous Trading Post supplied most productions.

A surprising consequence of the shift from traditional costume suppliers to military specialists, such as the famous Mollo dynasty and Brian Davis, mentioned earlier, along with a number of other recognized militaria collectors, is that standards of accuracy have gone up. Re-enactors are 'experts' who demand accuracy and, while Second World War blockbusters are like London buses, you wait for ages to see one and then two or three come along, re-enactors and professional educational outreach performers are the stock-in-trade of such suppliers. Enthusiasts like to recall the numerous inaccuracies in epics such as *The Longest Day* ('The Yanks are in green and the Krauts grey, that's good enough'), since the mid 1970s serious productions have been full of authenticity. Militaria buffs were amused by the accuracy of the life preservers equipping the US Rangers as they waded ashore on Omaha beach in *Saving Private Ryan*.

Although the rarity of authentic items has meant that the supply has fallen and prices risen, the development of the on-line market place has meant that the market has expanded enormously. The internet has affected things dramatically, and especially eBay. The international trade in militaria has progressed at a furious pace. However, the huge quantity offered by the electronic market place has proved a double-edged sword and is, in fact, destroying the supply, the lifeblood of the hobby.

Nevertheless, collecting is an addiction and we addicts are resigned to trawling through endless lists in the hope that, maybe, we might find a *Pickelhaube* mistakenly listed as a crash helmet or a parachutist's jump-bag – a most sought-after military collectable – listed as a second-hand sports equipment hold-all or as a 'green punch-bag'. It's a new golden age for collectors.

2 Collecting Passions

Before we look at the different types of military collectable, what's hot and what's not, and where to buy or sell such items, it is worth looking in detail at the British collectables scene. To understand the genesis of the current industry better it is useful to discover a little more about some of its colourful characters, such as Chris Farlowe, who played crucial roles in building it.

ROY SMITH

One collector who has straddled both the professional costumier's and the militaria enthusiast's world is Roy Smith. His story explains how the several elements of the hobby fused to create today's burgeoning militaria market, but, more importantly perhaps, it puts everything into context. Born in North London in 1942, Roy started collecting what he calls the 'detritus' of the Second World War by simply picking up the bits of shrapnel and spent cartridges that could still be found on bombsites. Apart from these, many schoolboys amassed a collection of souvenirs such as German badges, medals and even flags brought back as souvenirs by demobbed relatives. Significantly, Roy reckons that his interest in military things might have been a by-product of the Second World War and his own exposure to it. Indeed, he believes this is why there are so few young collectors today. We hope that this book helps to redress the balance.

By the age of ten Roy also possessed dozens of spent

Militaria enthusiast and expert collector Roy Smith photographed with a rare Second World War folding 'Parabike' as used by allied paratroops. Designed in 1941, more than 60,000 of these cycles were produced. They weighed only 21lb.

cartridge cases, plucked from the ranges at the nearby Hackney Marshes. Aware of his interests, a neighbour who had been in the Home Guard during the war presented him with more wartime treasures which he had kept in his garden shed since the end of hostilities. Then in his early teens Roy came across an antique shop in nearby Tottenham and started collecting in earnest.

> With my meagre pocket money I managed to buy things that took my fancy or, more correctly, items that I could afford. A common bayonet without a scabbard would cost about 2s.6d. (13p) and a small flintlock pistol £3. My collection of rather random items grew, but I did acquire several very fine pieces by today's standards.

At school Roy met others with similar collecting interests. They bought and exchanged items and soon discovered other dealers selling desirable collectables. 'At this time I did not know of any dedicated militaria dealers... The shops we visited were junk shops or general second-hand dealers who sold everything, fishing rods, air rifles and pistols, furniture, model railways, sporting goods.'

Everything changed in 1963, however, when Roy and his closest friend John discovered London's famous Portobello Road antiques market. Starting here, in West London's Notting Hill area, Roy and John established a precise routine to their Saturday militaria purchasing sprees. After visiting Portobello, particularly a cheaper section of it known as 'The Rough End', 'where real bargains could be found', they would chart a course eastwards through the myriad junk shops and markets of Marylebone and Soho. They generally finished their meanderings in Camden Passage, encountering along the way numerous dealers and characters now famous in the annals of military collectables.

> Until then collecting had been a rather solitary hobby. Now I found that there were serious collectors and dealers too! I became very friendly with one of the very early collector-dealers, Jim DeFelice, and got a job helping him on his stall on Saturdays. His house was literally filled with swords, old guns and daggers and we all aspired to having one like his!

Other dealers on the Portobello Road included such luminaries as Tony Oliver, Tom Greenaway (who later opened Blunderbuss Antiques in London's Thayer Street, which is still a haven for military enthusiasts), 'The Major', Adrian Foreman, George Kellam, Tom Stubbs and Alan Beadle. Portobello Road rapidly became the preferred Saturday meeting place for collectors. Yet other established dealers from this period included Peter Dredge and Eddie Kenten, who specialized in American Civil War items. At one time Roy was the proud owner of many rare and authentic items from the armies of both the North and the South. Roy showed us receipts for items purchased from North American dealers in the late 1960s – original tunic buttons purchased for pennies.

Roy recalled that 'Malcolm Fisher's shop Regimentals probably had the finest display of militaria at this time', and that 'Bill Tobin was one earliest German militaria dealers ... He was an old established dealer even in the 1960s. He opened his "shop" for

Article about the pop-singer and militaria dealer Chris Farlowe, from Titbits, *a popular weekly magazine from the 1960s, the forerunner of today's rash of 'celebrity' titles.*

business only on Saturday mornings at 10 o'clock sharp and was always on our Saturday route. He sold from what had once been a basement flat in a dingy Victorian south London tenement block. We, eager collectors, queued in the dark passageway that always smelt strongly of urine and disinfectant in equal measure. At ten he'd open the door and there would be a rush to see what new treasures he'd acquired. His prices were always fair and he did find some very rare items.'

The 1963 film by Kevin Brownlow and Andrew Mollo, *It Happened Here*, a British 'what if' production about a German invasion of Britain in 1940, featured many contemporary collectors in its cast, the dealers Tony Oliver and Bill Tobin famously played minor parts.

It was while in Camden Passage at the Angel, Islington – another popular 1960s antiques hub in London – that Roy met Chris Farlowe. The successful musician occupied the end portion of a friend's stall from where he sold militaria. 'He then expanded with several large stalls, or boutiques as they were known then, into the arcade and eventually had his own shop Call To Arms at 79 Upper Street.' Roy said that Farlowe's premises became a Mecca for collectors of German militaria in particular. 'Saturday would be rather like a collectors' club', he told me. 'Chris was a very popular singer and toured widely on the Continent. There he made many contacts and acquired many fine items for the shop. We would eagerly await his return from a trip and there would be much competition to get to see the new imports.' After a while Farlowe opened a shop in Hamburg, trading in fine and rare examples of Nazi memorabilia that had somehow survived the war, emerging from German cellars and secluded back rooms to be greeted by eager collectors.

In April 1968 an article in the regular 'A Piece of Our Mind' feature in the popular British weekly magazine *Titbits*, highlighted the pop star's unlikely obsession. Entitled 'Come off it, Chris, Hitlerism is no joke', the piece began, 'A £10,000 hoard of Nazi treasure lies tucked away in a North London alley. And it is watched over by a 28-year-old pop singer.' The article was written before Farlowe established Call to Arms. He was photographed in one of his Camden Passage premises, 'Chris Farlowe's Militaria Vault'. Clearly the journalist was intent on

exposing a darker side to the singer, 'who had delighted thousands of fans when his hit "Handbags and Gladrags" shot into the charts'. Farlowe, however, was no patsy, explaining that 'Certainly we've had cranks here, saluting Hitler's picture, but we throw 'em straight out.' However, he did say that it was getting much harder for him and his partner Jimmy Joslyn to source authentic Nazi uniforms. 'SS uniforms, now £60 each, are becoming rare', he said. (Times have changed!) 'In 1972 I went to work in the military department of Bermans & Nathans, in London's Leicester Square', Roy said. (Bermans' was then the largest television, film and theatrical costumiers in the world.) 'There I could put my knowledge of German and British uniforms to some commercial use. I was involved in many interesting productions, *Star Wars* being especially notable.'

The costume expert John Mollo was the wardrobe master for *Star Wars*. 'He came in to Bermans' and told me that he wanted some mock-ups to show the production team. So he and I found various bits of military equipment, modified it and, working from his design sketches, put together the characters that we are all familiar with. Darth Vader's helmet started out as a World War I German helmet.' Apparently all the items were taken away, further modified and, when approved by the designers, manufactured in the studio workshops. Mollo received an Oscar for costume design on *Star Wars*.

Roy was involved on many other productions, including *A Bridge Too Far*, *Tommy* and *Aces High*. 'It was interesting to meet the stars and production people', he recalled, 'and it was very satisfying to see your work on the screen.' He also worked on television programmes including *Dad's Army*, in one memorable episode of which a U-boat crew captured the entire Walmington-on-Sea Home Guard unit: 'I did the uniforms for the U-boat crew.' *It Ain't Half Hot Mum*, the Morecambe and Wise show, *Upstairs, Downstairs* and *Monty Python* also benefited from Roy's expert knowledge.

Until the early 1970s there were few detailed reference books on the subject of Third Reich militaria. Davis and Mollo were among the first authors to produce informative and accurate works and items from Roy's collection have appeared in their books.

Promotional flyer for Mike Ross's Quartermasters shop located in the Angel, Islington.

Having built up a considerable collection of militaria, in 1975 Roy married Monika, an art student. The couple moved out of London, with the consequence that, because Roy no longer mixed in the same circle, his collecting urge waned. Deciding that his collecting days were over at last, he sold his collection to several dealers and ventured into another field, classic motorcycles. These machines encouraged him to return to his original trade of engineering. Now semi-retired, he works occasionally for 'the legendary Nick Hall' of Sabre Sales in Portsmouth. Roy's activities include cataloguing and selling Sabre's goods on the internet. 'How times have changed', he mused.

MIKE ROSS

The late Mike Ross of Military Marine (later known Quartermasters at The Angel) was one of the most charismatic militaria dealers in the 1970s and the 1980s. Ross and Eddie Kenten (who was particularly interested in military vehicles) formed the BRA, the Battle Re-enactment Association, with the aim of supplying uniformed military 'extras' to the film industry. The pair also astutely realized that they could build an organization that would create a regular demand for the uniforms and insignia that Quartermasters sold. In reality, of course, enthusiasts do not always make the best film extras. How many overweight, *SS Standartenführers* were there anyway and how many American snipers with glasses?

Ross was one of the first collector-dealers who combed wholesalers' warehouses, realizing the value in much previously neglected surplus material ('It's got a label with a 1940–41 date stamp on it, so it must be of value to a collector'). Sadly, these repositories have long gone. WW II BRA (the irony was not lost on the founders; this is now known as The Second World War Living History Association) also organized spectacular public displays. The membership, composed of collectors and enthusiasts, would, it was hoped, always present themselves in the correct uniforms and equipment. On 6 May 1978, as a preliminary to the public displays, a private 'battle' took place at Charring in Kent. This event enabled Mike and Eddie to check the authenticity of the re-enactors involved and perhaps provide them with more suitable alternatives if they turned up shoddily dressed. Benefiting from the rehearsals at Charring, two months later Combat Promotions and the BRA staged their first public display. On 1 and 2 July 1978 'The Battle of Molash' took place at Bower Farm in Kent. It has since achieved near legendary status among first-generation re-enactors. The events at Molash were billed as the largest gathering of men and vehicles assembled in Europe for the purpose of re-enacting a Second World War battle.

The promotional literature made exciting reading: 'This is the first rally and battle re-enactment staged by the promoters on this type of scale. We hope that everybody that attends will have an enjoyable day out. Weather permitting (as usual) here are a few things to look out for.' The bright yellow flyer went on to list an array of entertainments. These included: moving vehicles, weapons demonstrations, a 'combat course between Yanks and Krauts' and a 'Jeep driving skill test'. At 2.00 p.m. there was a one-minute silence 'In honour of the fallen on both sides in World War 2'. The early 1970s were a much less litigious time than today. Public liability was not such a feature in the organizing outdoor events. In short, lots of pyrotechnics could be used _ if not quite in abandon, but in a much freer way they than they ever could now. 'Spectators view this event entirely at their own risk and no liability can be accepted by the organizers, their servants, agents or any other members for associate loss, personal or otherwise which may thereby be suffered.' The flyer went on to remind visitors that although, 'These vehicles were made for big heavy soldiers to jump all over, that was 35 years ago, and since then someone has put a lot of care, time and money into restoring them, so please do not get in any vehicles without the owner's permission.'

Roy Smith met Mike when the latter was selling a great deal of Americana, military items sold as fashion accessories to wear rather than to collectors, he was soon enlisted to handle stall bookings at Molash. He was also busily engaged organizing and booking utilities, catering services, and in the necessary provision of latrines. Despite sailing uncharted waters, BRA pulled off a huge success at Molash. In fact the event was so professionally staged that Arundel Film Productions Ltd, a commercial film company, became interested in the endeavours of the BRA. They had approached Mike and Eddie to make a film of the BRA in the forthcoming battle. The result, *It's All a Game*, was later produced and BRA members attended the preview in London's Wardour Street. But 'to my knowledge it has never been broadcast or commercially shown', said Roy.

However, *It's All a Game* did find a larger audience when it was the subject of an entire edition of the seminal military enthusiasts' magazine *After the Battle*. The periodical featured numerous top quality photographs of scenes from the epic. Dick Budgen, of the film SFX specialists Action Incorporated, was hired to ensure first-class action stunts. Explosive charges, more

Combat Promotions and B.R.A.
PRESENTS
THE BATTLE OF
MOLASH
plus Historic Military
Rally and Display

1-2 July 1978

BOWER FARM, MOLASH, KENT.

RIGHT: Promotional flyer detailing the Battle Re-enactment Association's famous 'Battle of Molash' in 1978. This event was the forerunner of large-scale, open-air re-enactments of the kind popularized today by annual events such as the War & Peace Show at Beltring in Kent.

BELOW RIGHT: Another promotional piece from Mike Ross (when he ran the shop Military and Marine), which further dispels the myth that militaria enthusiasts are reclusives.

familiar in Hollywood than in the Garden of England, were used to dramatic effect, hurling stuntmen skyward as they detonated. Ross's own American Stuart 5a/1 light tank was filmed crushing an 'enemy' staff car. Readers may be interested to learn that this AFV actually featured in the classic movie *The Dirty Dozen*, starring alongside Lee Marvin. It is worth mentioning that, contrary to being the 'anoraks' some may assume, many of the 1960s' militaria buffs, including the ex-art student Mike Ross and his then girlfriend the former Bunny Girl Patty McClenahan, were quite media savvy. Slick publicity, high quality photography and motion camera work were all well within their capabilities.

The 'Battle of Molash' was the first event of its kind, presenting authentic Second World War re-creations with professionalism and style. Its success inspired members of a Kent-based military vehicle club The Invicta Military Vehicle Preservation Society (IMPS) to stage similar spectacles.

After approaching the Whitbread brewery in 1987, IMPS was given permission to hold its first event on the firm's Kent hop farm. A hundred and fifty original Second World War military vehicles attended the two-day spectacular. Today, the famous War and Peace Show at Beltring Hop Farm is spread over three days and attracts up a thousand classic military vehicles.

NICK HALL

And now to Nick Hall. No account of the military collectables hobby would be complete without mentioning this affable, larger-than-life character. Nick Hall, a collector of arms and armour since childhood was considered so unusual in the 1950s that he was featured in the BBC children's programme *All Your Own*. Interviewed by Huw Weldon, Hall explained the ins and outs of his hobby and displayed the charismatic charm that has been a hallmark of his personality ever since. While serving in the Bermuda Police in the 1960s, he continued to collect antique

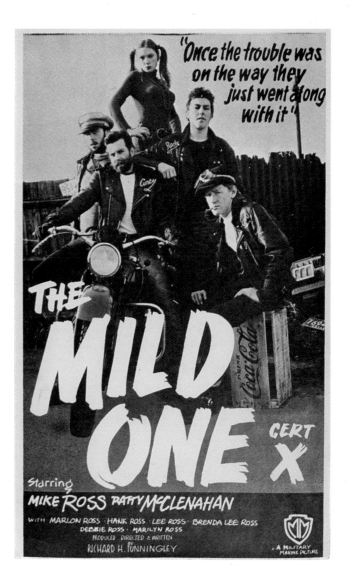

"Once the trouble was on the way they just went along with it"

THE
**MILD
ONE**
CERT
X

Starring
MIKE ROSS PATTY McCLENAHAN
WITH MARLON ROSS · HANK ROSS · LEE ROSS · BRENDA LEE ROSS
DEBBIE ROSS · MARILYN ROSS
PRODUCED DIRECTED & WRITTEN
BY RICHARD H. FUNNINGLEY

A MILITARY
MARINE PICTURE

arms. On his return to the United Kingdom in 1970 he continued to pursue his passion for historic weapons and accoutrements, joining a military collectors' society in the garrison town of Aldershot. Soon he began to wheel and deal in the pursuit of his hobby, quickly gaining a reputation as someone who knew where to procure collectable militaria. By his own admission, Hall purchased almost anything that took his fancy. However, he also displayed the single-minded focus that has been such a success for him in business, quickly establishing an enviable collection of British Imperial full dress uniforms and headdresses.

He was known for locating rare and unusual British insignia in the most obscure places and was also adept at scouring the dusty storage spaces in the premises of the original manufacturers or the military tailors. Through contacts made while serving in Bermuda, Hall was one of the first in Britain to import American insignia and military equipment direct from its manufacturers, quartermasters and even PX (post exchange) retail units.

In the late 1970s, as interest among military enthusiasts began to focus increasingly on the uniforms and equipment of the Second World War and among re-enactors and military vehicle enthusiasts, classic machines such as Willy's jeeps, M3 halftracks and 6 ¥ 6 lorries, Hall took part in the growing number of live events and began to trade more actively with fellow enthusiasts. In fact, the sale and exchange of military collectables became such an important part of his life that in September 1988 be took the plunge and decided to pursue his hobby with

The legendary Nick Hall, proprietor of Portsmouth's Sabre Sales, in typically understated pose.

gusto, opening his shop, Sabre Sales, in Southsea's Castle Street. This quickly became a focal point for south-coast collectors and the rest, as they say, is history. Like many of his competitors, Hall realized that, with a finite supply of authentic military collectables available, it would eventually become impossible to find affordable examples of historic military equipment. Furthermore, the impact of on-line sales and the power of eBay to drain further what few original items there were, meant that to survive commercially, Sabre Sales had to diversify. Consequently, Nick's business is now divided between the sale of authentic military collectables and the temporary hire of military outfits. Fortunately, the number of significant military anniversaries in recent years as the media and individuals have realized that, with the passing of time, such momentous events as D-Day and VE and VJ Days deserved to be celebrated, has meant a ready demand for period dress.

During his career Hall has met a wide range of individuals associated with the world of military collectables. To prosper in what is, anyway, a 'people' business in every sense, you have to build a reputation for trust and fairness, not just with your customers, but also with other dealers and specialists. Networking is all-important. In the field of military collectables one's good name goes a long way and, although dealers are obviously in business to make a profit, the world they inhabit, built upon a foundation of eager enthusiasts and trusted specialists, depends more on someone's word and the promise in a firm handshake than many might expect.

But like Nick, whom, once met, will never be forgotten, the world of militaria has always been inhabited by colourful personalities. When still a youth he recalls another legendary character who traded from Brighton's famous 'caves'. Known by everyone simply as 'Grafton', this gentleman kept an armourclad figure seated on a horse as a talking point for those who visited his shop. Apparently, Grafton dealt in nineteenth-century bayonets 'by the bucket-load' and sold nineteenth-century Austrian muskets 'for £7 mint'.

A local collector and contemporary of Nick's was R.V. Barrett of Gosport, who started collecting militaria in the 1940s. His penchant was for firearms and he had a copy of every single British service rifle used by the Crown's forces since they were first issued. Much of his collection Barrett bought at London's famous Caledonian Road market. Despite the rarity even then of the items he sought, he allegedly never paid more than £10 for a single item. How modern collectors must weep! Another kindred spirit who also shared Hall's passion for collectables was Hooper of Croxley Green. His primary interest was in ethnographic weapons – those used by developing peoples, the spears, swords and bows used by the indigenous peoples of Africa, the Middle East and. This is a topic about which Nick Hall is an acknowledged expert; he often exchanged information and sought the answer to a particular query about some arcane fighting instrument with Hooper in the 1950s who was one of the greatest collectors in this interesting and important field.

The first really significant collector of material from the Third Reich recalled by Nick was another prominent name from the early years of the hobby – Lt Col C.M. Dodkins; formerly of the 3rd Carabiniers, Dodkins held the DSO and was central to the modern development of the military collectables hobby. And yet another prominent character from the early days of Hall's career was J.A. Morrison, an ex-RAOC major. Apparently, one day Morrison, who still had useful contacts in the military establishment, received a call from the War Office saying that,

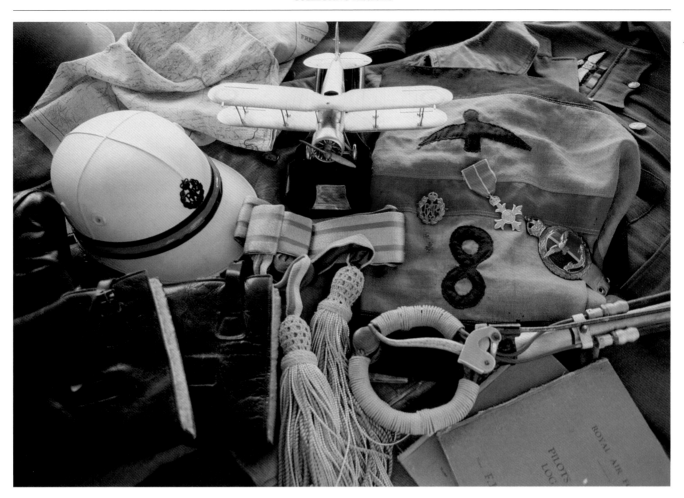

ABOVE: *Cross-section of RAF uniform, headdress insignia and ephemeral items, including a 1918 pre-blue khaki officer's uniform, 1950s motorcycle helmet for RAF police; First World War flying coat; early Second World War flying boots, silk escape map, officer's No.1 dress belt, pilots log books and an aircraft control stick.*

BELOW: *Selection of Second World War 'Sweetheart' badges and pins. Most of these items are quite collectable, especially the 'Upper Thames Patrol' Home Guard badge, RAF silver sweetheart wings, Women's Land Army pin-back enamel badge for wear on uniforms and the ARP enamel lapel badge.*

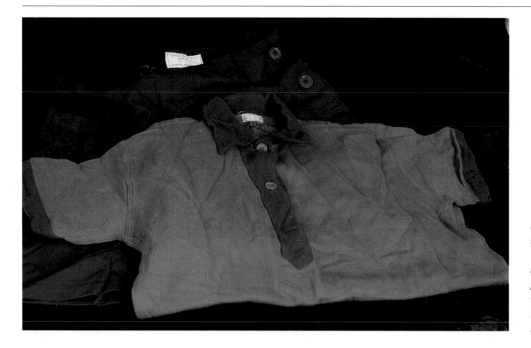

Second World War ATS physical training top and shorts. First issued in 1943, the orange and brown colours are those of the ATS. Brown Aertex gym knickers were also produced to be worn under the 'shorts, divided'. Importantly for collectors, the item labels and date can be clearly seen.

although he was no longer with the colours, those in authority felt that he could be trusted to help the army to dispose of unwanted items. He agreed, and the first lot he was contracted to distribute among dealers and collectors made his fortune and his reputation. The consignment the War Office needed help to dispose of? Its entire stocks of .303-calibre sniper rifles. This deal secured Morrison's reputation for knowing where to locate and procure interesting and potentially valuable British military surplus to such an extent that, by the late 1960s, he was contracted to provide the producers of *The Charge of the Light Brigade* with issue troopers' overalls and accoutrements.

Another story concerns another equally prominent, William Tobin. In the 1950s there was resurgence in the activities of Oswald Mosley's British Union of Fascists. Apparently Tobin's Portobello Road shop did a roaring trade supplying items of Nazi

memorabilia to BUF members attending the numerous London rallies. And another trader recalled by Nick was Tom Greenaway, a name familiar to all those who have collected militaria during recent times. Being short of stature, Greenaway, who served with the 2nd Battalion Coldstream Guards just after the Second World War, had the honour of being on the receiving end of one of legendary RSM Brittain's loud tirades. Brittain, famous for having the loudest bark in the British army, considered Greenaway too short and, calling him a 'shitehawk', did his best to force the hapless Guardsman's transfer to another battalion. But Greenaway had the last laugh, after he retired from the service and established his military collectables business, Blunderbuss Antiques in London's Thayer Street, Greenaway received a call from Moss Bros. In the early 1980s offering him, at a knock-down price a huge supply of unclaimed army uni-

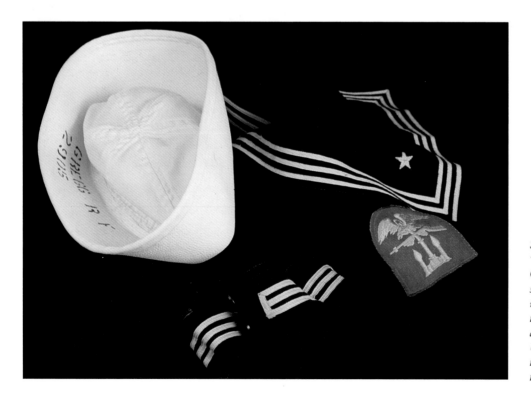

Second World War US Navy rating's 'blue top' with Navy Combined Operations patch on left sleeve (note the stars and stripes motif on the collar rear). Complete with sailors' white cotton 'gob' hat, devised as a working dress hat but most commonly worn by US sailors at other times rather than the stiff, blue 'Donald Duck' traditional sailors' cap.

*Layout of a Royal Navy rating's uniform items from Second World War, specifically illustrating the type of size and date labels
to be found on the issue Square Rig uniform. Illustration includes blue and white tropical money-belts, a pair of ratings' issue
boots and other ephemeral items. These are all arranged on a red and yellow signal flag.*

forms and headdresses, all of the highest quality.

Hall remembers numerous characters who each, in his individual way, made the modern hobby what it is: Dougie Squires, who dealt in cap badges and buttons from the Sussex hamlet of Bury; Terry 'Trader' Grey, based in Aldershot in the 1960s and selling Victorian blue cloth helmets, in their original storage tins, for the princely sum of £3.50. Further afield Nick recalls a visit to Montreal in 1964 and, happening upon a store known simply and appropriately as General Surplus. Here he spied 'crate upon crate' of British-made, First World War other ranks' trench caps all selling for Canadian $10 each. Today, if you could still procure them, these items of headgear would be worth hundreds of pounds.

JOE LYNDHURST
Before we look in detail at the categories of military collectables and consider aspects such as preservation and display, we should not finish our survey of British collectors without mentioning the late Joe Lyndhurst. Born in 1924, Joe was one of the pioneering militaria collectors in Britain. He was also especially significant in the development here of the classic military vehicle hobby. However, he is perhaps best known for his famous Warnham War Museum and for writing that most valuable resource of militaria collectors, *Military Collectables* (Salamander Books, 1983). During the Second World War he had been intrigued by the jeeps that he saw driven by Canadian and American soldiers and decided that he wanted to own one. It took him until 1962 when he bought his first from a film company. He bought others, entering three into the Brighton Run in 1968 and taking all three prizes in the military class.

Joe and his family ran the New Beach Holiday Camp at Earnley, near Chichester. Fortunately, this site provided him with storage for his growing collection of military vehicles and off-season was a venue used for gatherings of like-minded military vehicle enthusiasts. When the holiday camp was sold in 1974, he bought 'Tyldens', near Horsham, turning it into the Warnham War Museum, which opened at Easter 1976. Gatherings there soon acquired near-legendary status among enthusiasts and the site began to host monthly militaria sales and auctions.

Arthur Ward noted in his recent book *Classic Kits* that the SAS jeep displayed at Warnham was once visited by designers and draughtsmen from the famous Japanese construction kit firm Tamiya. It is interesting to learn that the famous 1/35th-scale replica of this desert warrior was based on the one that for so long resided in Joe's museum. Over time the collections outgrew even the substantial premises at Warnham and he was forced to sell. Following an illness, Joe died in 2000. Fittingly, however, at the War and Peace show in 2005 he was awarded *After the Battle*'s Bart Vanderveen Challenge Shield for his activities at Warnham and in the classic military vehicle hobby.

3 Insignia

Military badge and medal collecting has always been one of the most popular military collectables sectors. Most of us suffer from space and storage restrictions but, fortunately, a relatively large accumulation of metal and cloth insignia takes up little space. Although nothing much has changed as regards the most coveted regimental or arm of service insignia – and we shall look at this in detail below – a more recent trend as regards medals has been the popularity of post-Second World War awards. Like those issued during the First World War, these feature the name of the recipient. Consequently medals awarded for service in Bosnia, Iraq or Afghanistan, for example are eminently collectable.

THE DEVELOPMENT OF INSIGNIA

Apart from the heraldic devices originating in the eleventh century adorning shields, tabards and later banners, probably the earliest form of battlefield emblem was the standard. This large and colourful flag was visible amid the smoke and confusion of combat and was used to indicate a rallying point; troops literally followed the colours.

The first systematic 'insignia' which could identify individual units date back to Cromwell's time. Regulation was the order of the day in the New Model Army and soldiers wore standardized garb and could expect regular pay. Along with the distinctive lobster-pot helmet and buff coatee, its soldiers enjoyed the first flowerings of the kind of group identification which has contributed to the *esprit-de-corps* the British army has for so long taken for granted. But, nevertheless, the rival armies on the battlefield could still be difficult to distinguish and it was not until 1660, eleven years after the civil war ended, that the restoration of Charles II saw the creation of a regular standing army. However, even then commanding officers enjoyed great licence as to how they dressed and equipped their soldiers. But it needed the Duke of Cumberland's reforms in 1747 before a regularized system was introduced of numbering individual regiments, indicating the precedence of each in relation to the others. In 1751 a royal warrant first introduced the term 'badge', metal insignia initially appearing on leather cartridges. A clothing warrant of 1768 regularized the positioning of metal badges for grenadiers on their bearskin caps.

Insignia in their modern sense were not fully adopted by armies until well into the latter half of the eighteenth century

Broad-spectrum layout of military insignia awards and headdress, including a Second World War peaked cap belonging to a British staff colonel (note the red band); King's Royal Rifle Corps khaki beret of the same period; British cap badges: a general's, Queen's Regiment, Royal Scots, Manchesters, Second World War *Free Polish, RFC, German First World War Iron Cross 2nd Class, German belt buckle, Austro-Hungarian European medals and a First World War Prussian Pickelhaube plate.*

Royal Naval Headdress insignia 1940s: RM plate for white pith (Brunswick Star), RN officer's metal beret badge, RM other ranks cap and beret badge.

Detail of RM other ranks helmet plate with King's crown, motto: 'Per mare, Per Terre' ('By Sea, By Land') and battle honour 'Gibraltar'.

when elaborate peaked turbans and Tarletons (See the headdress worn by Col Sir Banastre Tarleton in the portrait of him by Sir Joshua Reynolds in the National Gallery.) were adorned with metal badges. Shakos (tall, cylindrical headdresses copied from the Austrians, who had copied the design from the Magyars) were introduced in 1800; these 8in-tall 'stovepipes' featuring large plates depicting unit insignia and adorned with plumes denoting regular, light or grenadier companies, quickly replaced the surviving mitres and tricorns. Headdresses were supplemented by gorgets and pewter buttons showing the number of each regiment. This period also saw the introduction of devices such as shoulder boards identifying ranks; previously status was identifiable only by the quality and cut of the uniform or the type and prestige of weapons, either of which would have identified officer rank. By the nineteenth century everything had become systematized to the extent that the concept of individual units being identified by name and number and soldiers by standardized emblems of rank and service arm was internationally accepted.

British armies, however, were different from those of other nations in one important aspect. Britain was the only country that, since Edward Cardwell's reforms of 1868, had concentrated on establishing precise regional bounds within its soldiery (not merely a number). Consequently, scripted/heraldic provincial identities were adopted rather than the organizing of units solely by a less emotive numbering system.

The then Secretary of State for War Hugh Childers, whose reforms came into effect in 1881, continued to strengthen county affiliations by discarding the numeral system and combining most of the single-battalion regiments into two-battalion regiments with, for the most part, county names in their titles. This created a force of sixty-nine line infantry regiments, consisting of forty-eight English, ten Scottish, eight Irish, and three Welsh regiments. The British discovered that men fought with

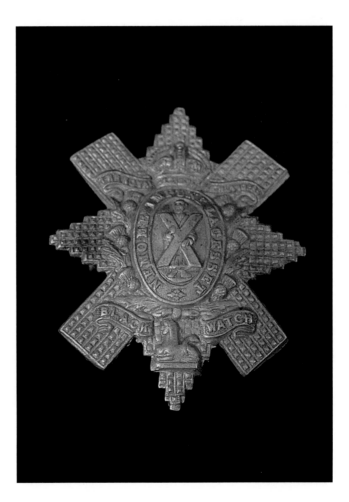

Second World War Royal Highlanders (Black Watch) Badge for Glengarry; unusually, during the twentieth century regular battalions when in the field did not normally wear this, instead they would opt to wear the red feather hackle on the tam-o'-shanter.

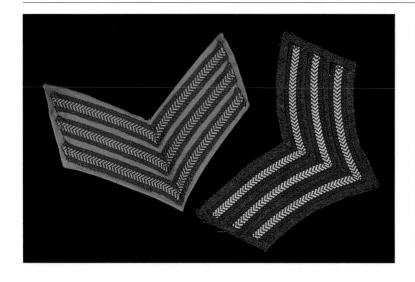

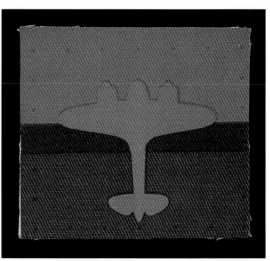

Khaki British sergeant's stripes as worn on service and battledress; the khaki drill version was worn on tropical uniforms.

Printed Air Liaison Signals patch.

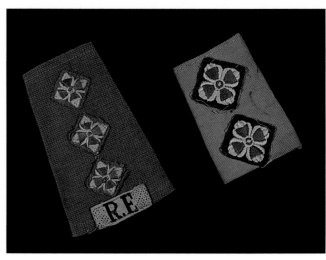

Great War British cloth Insignia: Suffolk Regiment embroidered slip-on is an economy measure introduced to replace existing brass shoulder titles, they were designed to be attached to tunic epaulettes although it was not unknown for them to be stitched to the top of the sleeve. The 'Bombers' qualification badge was awarded to personnel trained to be effective in the use of the standard British hand-grenade, the Mills bomb.

Two Second World War vintage British officer's slip-on rank slides. One in jungle green (JG) for a captain, Royal Engineers (left), probably of Indian manufacture and (right) in khaki drill (KD) for a lieutenant (Royal Engineers, blue pips).

Edward VII Yeomanry officer's pouch badge with frosted finish.

Selection of Second World War RAF cloth insignia: 'padded' pilot's wings; navigator's half-wing (unpadded); embroidered airman's sleeve eagle; embroidered RAF Regiment shoulder title and printed leading aircrafts-man's (LAC) rank badge.

vigour if they were part of the 'Gloucesters', 'the Wessex Regiment' or 'the East Kents', and not simply identified as the '4th Regiment of Foot'.

Perhaps the most famous Secretary of State for War was R.B. Haldane (later Viscount Haldane of Cloan). His reforms of 1907–08 saw the creation of the Imperial General Staff under a senior officer who was the Chief of the Imperial General Staff. Under his direction, the army also took stock of the changes in fighting heralded by the quick-firing, bolt-action rifle and use of camouflage, cover and even wide-brimmed slouch hats, used to such good effect by Boer troops during the South African War of

1902. However, the twentieth century was a harbinger of new techniques of war and key aspects of the mechanized battlefield led to further developments in military insignia.

The introduction of khaki uniforms and shrapnel helmets dictated by the trench warfare of the First World War necessitated the adoption of what were originally called 'battle patches' on British uniforms. With no insignia on helmets and shoulder titles being distinguishable at distance, these cloth devices readily identified battalions or brigades within a division, thus enabling commanders to make battlefield dispositions without the need to be among the front-line fighting. However, the

First World War selection showing a RNAS armoured car cap badge, a Light Infantry officer's cap boss and a Prussian regimental emblem.

First World War British cap badges and collar insignia; cap badges: Machine Gun Corps, Ox and Bucks OTC, Women's Land Army (WLA), 3rd Carabiniers, 14th Battalion (Young Citizens) The Royal Irish Rifles; collar badges: Duke of Cornwall's Light Infantry ('One For All'), Duke of Wellington's Regiment (West Riding).

introduction of such patches quickly engendered displays of unit loyalty – the 51st 'Highland' Division, for example, and went some way towards ameliorating the depersonalization of modern warfare. The armies of Germany and France, for example, did not need to adopt the allied system of battle patches; their uniforms sported clear unit numbers on tunic collars supplemented by piping (*Waffen Farbe*) on collars and shoulder boards denoting the arm of service.

In Britain at the end of the First World War many of the enormous array of insignia that had crept back on to combat uniforms were to be removed. The new British battledress pattern introduced in 1939 was designed with homogeneous simplicity in mind. It was considered an important aspect of field security that a captured soldier, bearing no markings, would not reveal his unit and consequently the dispositions of allied troops. Slip-on shoulder boards could be removed within the battlefield area and black or green buttons would replace shiny brass ones. However, the purpose and the spirit of the new uniforms were somewhat undermined by the end of 1940 with the adoption of visible, coloured, field service flashes. By 1941 this adornment had been augmented by the adoption of divisional and, in some cases, regimental flashes. By the end of the war, soldiers wore a wide range of insignia denoting their rank, regiment, division, trade and qualification (often produced in regimental colours, that is, for example, black on green for rifle regiments and black on red for the King's Royal Rifle Corps), war-service chevrons, campaign ribbons and, in some cases, even regimental lanyards. The designers of the futuristically streamlined, new battledress could only weep.

Twentieth-century wars also encouraged the development of often quite small units, now collectively known as 'special forces'. These adopted specific cloth insignia to describe their roles or capabilities. The American armies were the fastest to move away from metal cap badges, which were usually national, and collar insignia, which generally denoted unit affiliations, in favour of a plethora of cloth patches to describe their numerous units.

COLLECTING INSIGNIA

Because of the number and variety of badges, both metal and cloth, the collecting of insignia is easily accessible to the enthusiast. In the broadest terms, the desirability and value of either a cloth or a metal badge stems from the association with whoever wore it and when. Even though the insignia of the Third Reich have always commanded the best prices, the value of a *Waffen* [armed] *SS* item compares poorly with a badge belonging to the Reich's forestry commission or the Todt organization (builders of the defensive strong points and anti-tank defences protecting the perimeter of the 'Thousand Year Reich'). But here's the conundrum: the forestry commission, for example, would be a much smaller organization than the *Waffen SS*, which, at its height, consisted of many hundreds of thousands of soldiers. Consequently, as regards their value for collectors, it is the insignia of the Reich's nurserymen, tree surgeons and lumber jacks which are the rarer. But generally collectors, initially at least, are minded to seek out the badges worn by fighting troops. Indeed, today many militaria collectors of thirty or more years' standing possess valuable collections of rare Nazi party regalia, SA badges and Reich Chancellery administrative insignia, for example, built up because, in the days when dealers still had plentiful stocks of authentic Second World war militaria, few purchasers chose them. Now everyone wants an *SA* dagger or even an official Nazi Party lapel pin.

Third Reich regalia still tops the popularity charts and, for a price, collectors can find examples of almost anything they desire. But think about it – at the peak of the *Wehrmacht*'s operations Hitler had 9 million men under arms. This figure represents a huge quantity of uniforms, badges and military equipment. One would expect much of it to have survived. However, for the losers of any war it is not exactly a level playing field. For the Germans untainted by fascism, their armies were considered to be a manifestation of political evil, not just of militarism. After the war the process of 'denazification' effectively removed all traces of fascist imagery, especially objects that bore the swastika (which, of course, most Third Reich insignia did). At the end of the war, German troops entering a prison

Selection of British Second World War cloth qualification, unit and field service insignia: parachute wings and parachute-trained badges, tank crewman, machine gunner; motorcyclist; physical training instructor (crossed swords, PTI); 5th Anti-Aircraft Division, 43rd Wessex (printed), grey and yellow embroidered Army Catering Corps field service strip, set of three embroidered red infantry seniority strips.

US Insignia: cloth 17th Airborne Division (Rhine Crossing); 6th Armoured Division (17th and 6th both of US manufacture); 9th Infantry Division (served in north-west Europe and probably 'theatre-made' in the UK); late war corporal's stripe worn both on field and Class 'A' uniforms; group of three overseas service bars, each representing one year's service; US Army second lieutenant brass and captain's silver bars (typical of Second World War period with long bar pins used for attachment to uniforms rather than the later short pins and clutch covers); enlisted soldier's collar disc for the medical branch (example shown is of late war manufacture with short pin and clutch cover attachment; frosted gilt officer's service cap badge (unusual in being produced in the UK by J.R. Gaunt).

laager would systematically have their insignia removed and destroyed. Most returning soldiers living in the Soviet-occupied zone hurriedly destroyed anything that could have associated them with Hitler's regime. Families at home were as eager to rid themselves of any party icons. In the American zone GIs organized street events based around huge bonfires on which badges and military and Nazi propaganda materials were ceremonially burned. In consequence not much survived. Yet, during the sixty years since the end of the war, the collectors' marketplace has been full of examples of almost every badge variant from each of the three armed services. Many are obviously fakes.

Although a healthy and mostly honest repro market thrives today, for re-enactors and historic military vehicle enthusiasts primarily wanting something that looks right without its necessarily being rare and original, the financial incentive is more than enough encouragement for counterfeiters. With *Waffen SS* tunics selling for £1,000 plus, it makes commercial sense to commission a tailor to fabricate a copy of a 1940s uniform item. In a sense, the enthusiasts have shot themselves in the foot. Demanding ever more reference material, collectors of militaria and scale modellers have encouraged the growth of a massive publishing industry, providing reference books detailing every conceivable uniform and regalia configuration worn by the soldiers of nearly all the world's armies. So, there is plenty of authoritative source material for forgers to copy, ensuring that their reproductions are accurate enough to fool even the most

ABOVE: A German Second World War medal with cover slip as issued, presented to workers on the Atlantic wall.

LEFT: A brass German Second World War RAD (Reichsarbeitsdienst, National Labour Service) plaque ('Work is noble').

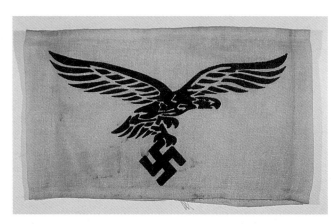

Second World War Luftwaffe brassard.

A Nazi Party member's armband; this is an embroidered version but it also exists in screen-printed form.

A Volkssturm armband; the Volkssturm were the Third Reich's equivalent of Britain's Home Guard and, by the war's end, comprised mostly boys and old men fighting desperately in the rubble of a ruined Germany.

A Luftwaffe other rank's eagle and roundel for the M43 ski cap.

ABOVE: A Second World War German army officer's breast eagle in silver Bevo weave; other ranks' versions were green or grey.

RIGHT: A Hitler Youth bronze sports award pin, Deutsches Jungvolk Leistungabzeichen (German Young Person's Performance Badge); this lapel pin was a small version of a much larger award.

knowledgeable. Conversely, although the current volume of reference material has definitely enriched the hobby, enabling collectors to see individual items in the context of complete uniforms, and uniforms and equipments in the contexts of their functions on campaign, these materials have proved essential to the counterfeiter.

Demand fuels supply. If someone is prepared to part with hard-earned cash for an item they have long desired, the coveted item will be provided. Although most collectors seek examples of militaria in the best condition, the scarcity of authentic items means that even damaged or fragmentary badges and military equipments are saleable. Indeed, today there is a thriving market in 'battlefield archaeology' – the excavation of buried combat relics. This has long been the case with aviation enthusiasts, who have disinterred crumpled airframes in southern England dating back to the Battle of Britain. Today, it seems that even

Selection of Third Reich insignia and ephemera: tank crewman's skull cap badge, metal eagle/swastika shield and national colours shield for Afrika Korps pith helmet, Feldgendarmerie (military police) gorget, RAD (Reichsarbeitsdienst) brass door plaque, miniature booklet ('Battle in the East'), party armband and a rare standard top from an NSKOV flag; the National Socialist Kriegsopferverein was the Wehrmacht's old comrades' association.

ABOVE: Selection of Second World War German Air Force insignia with Luftwaffe dagger. Includes breast eagle cloth and metal pilot badge, observer's badge, other ranks' belt buckle, signaller's badge, silver wire lanyard. The dagger features an amber (yellow) plastic hilt to match the Waffenfarbe of flying personnel and paratroops, it is shown with both belt hangers and silver wire knot; daggers complete with hangers and knots command the highest prices.

BELOW: A selection of items belonging to Pte Josef Busold and his family, including his Second World War German infantry assault badge and award citation; his Iron Cross 2nd Class, identity disc, miniature stick-pin of awards, a bullet head removed from the battlefield and a piece of the shrapnel with which Busold was wounded. The 'Mutter Kreuze' (mother's cross) belonged to his mother.

ABOVE: *Layout of British and Commonwealth badges including: bronze cap badges for officers – Queen's, Army Service Corps (of Great War vintage, winning the 'Royal' prefix in 1921 and becoming the RASC); metal line infantry cap badges – Buffs, Royal Fusiliers, Suffolk's, East Yorkshire's, Black Watch, Volunteer Battalion Post Office Rifles, Second World War plastic economy badges – Royal Artillery (bomb), Royal Engineers, Durham Light Infantry, King's Royal Rifle Corps, Devonshire Regiment; corps badges – Royal Artillery, Royal Engineers, RASC, REME, ATS; foreign and Commonwealth – Australian Commonwealth Military Forces, Free Dutch Volunteers (Second World War); miscellaneous – Royal Marine other ranks' helmet plate, RM other ranks' cap badge, RN officer's beret badge, badge of the Palestine Police.*

Home Guard printed shoulder title, area badge (Sussex) and unit number.

corroded army buttons and cap badges have a monetary value far beyond their apparent worth. As with all collectables, provenance is all-important and so, if an artefact can be proved to have been located on the site of a First or Second World War battlefield, its value will increase accordingly.

There is, however, one area of the repro market that is of value to collectors and within which articles are imbued with a unique sense of provenance: film and television props. An item that can be proved to have featured in classic war films such as *633 Squadron*, *The Battle of Britain*, *Patton*, *A Bridge Too Far* or *Saving Private Ryan*, for example, is often of a higher value than the authentic item it mimics. Furthermore, if there is evidence of celebrity association – proof that Clint Eastwood, Richard Burton or Tom Hanks wore the jacket or helmet, for example, this further enhances the value. However, such film-related items are beyond the scope of this book, entering as they do the thriving world of film and television memorabilia, where, as they say, art mimics life.

With both typical forms of insignia, cloth or metal, cheap and fairly obvious copies abound. The more sophisticated ones tend to be made of items that would, in any case, be of high value, such as American pilots' silver wings, rare Third Reich breast badges and the limited edition insignia manufactured for

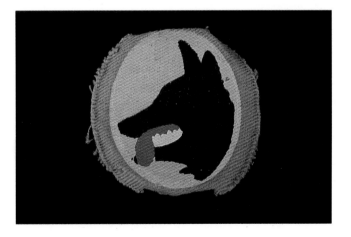

Sussex District, South-Eastern Command Home Guard unit flash.

Typical LDV (Local Defence Volunteer) brassard from the summer of 1940, often issued in lieu of uniform. Because the LDV was short-lived, Churchill thinking that 'Home Guard' was more stirring, such items are quite rare.

Set of Home Guard printed cloth insignia post-1942, showing both shoulder title unit area LON (London) and unit number.

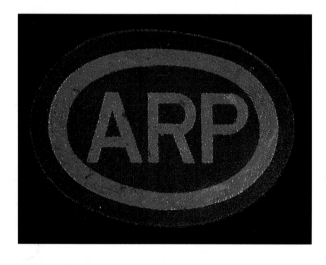

Unusual screen-printed ARP cloth badge for wear on male or female overalls during the early war period.

Printed ARP brassard. Early war period before the change to 'Civil Defence' (CD) and introduction of proper uniforms; this is a more common form although there are many other variants produced by local authorities and specific to an area or operational duty.

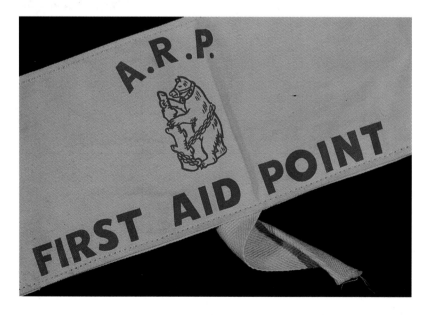

An AFS (Auxiliary Fire Service) cloth embroidered tunic badge for the London area, dating from the earlier part of Second World War.

More unusual and more desirable printed ARP brassard for the first aid personnel of Warwickshire.

and worn by special forces troops. It is worth faking an item that a collector expects to pay highly for. If even an authentic badge is worth only £15 to £20 there is naturally not much incentive to spend too much time and effort on the fake. A common feature of a reproduced item sold as real is that it has been artificially aged. This can be hard to detect, but the smell and the patina can never be entirely accurately simulated. The other major falsification involves the alteration of the location of mounting lugs or their removal entirely from helmet plates to suggest erroneously that they fitted another item of headdress. Often the combination of two items that would previously never have been combined can fraudulently create an item of improbable value.

It is appropriate to add here a note on the lugs, pins and fixtures of cap and collar badges. Original items reveal a continuation of surface finish and tone that a badge with a recently soldered pin can never suggest. Do not let anyone trick you into believing that an example of remedial work on a badge or other similar item was a 'field repair'. In their day badges and items of military equipment were cheap, purely utilitarian pieces – when they broke or went missing they were replaced, if possible, from the quartermaster's stores. Combat infantrymen certainly did not waste time mending insignia. The things to look out for are: a change in the surface finish of a metal item, suggesting that it

Women's Voluntary Service (WVS) embroidered sleeve brassard. The chevrons denote four years' war service.

is the marriage of two different items; evidence of solder, file marks and, worst of all, adhesive. Unless they are fresh from dark storage, period cloth items should exhibit some evidence of colour fading; items that have supposedly been worn in combat without any trace of stitch marks, holes or thread have clearly never been affixed to a uniform and, lastly but not least, any synthetic thread, such as nylon in any badge during or before the

The Royal Navy: red on black working uniform ('No.3 Dress') naval rating's trade or branch badge showing crossed flags denoting 'signaller' ('a bunting tosser') and single propeller of two 'star' value indicating a qualified mechanic (similar insignia depicting both branch and rank for petty officers and ratings also existed but these were manufactured from embroidered gold wire on black for best uniforms and embroidered and printed blue on white for tropical uniforms); printed war service chevrons worn on lower right sleeve (each representing one year of service in wartime – the same system being used by the army, RAF and civil defence personnel); officer's

shoulder boards for a captain RN and lieutenant commander Air Branch (indicated by letter 'A' in the centre of the 'executive loop'). These emblems illustrate both the standard gold lace and war-expedient working dress embroidered formats. The boards were worn either on tropical white or officers' battledress working uniforms, the official version of which was introduced in 1943; set of Fleet Air Arm officers' gold wire pilot wings; RN officer's cap badge, this is a more unusual version showing the crown and laurels made from gilded, pressed metal rather than the more typical embroidered gold wire.

Second World War (apart from certain American insignia), is probably not original.

Probably the only types of military collectable of interest to the re-enactor, which, by necessity, rely on the integration of certain non-original components, are classic military vehicles. Some, but not all, surviving military classics are owned as extensions of an enthusiast's miltaria collection rather than for love of their mechanical construction. A functioning period military vehicle or aircraft will always be a compromise of original parts, painstaking restoration and the necessity to use modern replacement items such as batteries, bulbs, tyres, canvas fittings and hoses.

Many smaller unit badges, generally of cloth, were locally made so the quality does vary. Often operational units of the RAF were temporarily based, for example, at a desert airfield or an advanced flying ground hastily fabricated to support the build up for the D Day landings. These units often adopted means of identification specific to their temporary locations. However, because a limited amount of these were produced, they were all mostly worn in theatre, which only adds to their value. Possibly the organizations requiring the smallest quantities of insignia, but which are of the greatest value to collectors, are those of the many special forces or 'private armies' that sprang up following Churchill's order to the Special Operations Executive (SOE) to 'Set Europe ablaze!'. Collectors have seldom been sure whether a regular army cap badge ever left the United Kingdom. On the other hand, the owners of Long Range Desert Group (LRDG) or Vietnam special forces insignia can be generally sure that, because so few were required and consequently produced, those that were made were worn in theatre.

As early as the 1960s repro material appeared in antique shops to be sold as original. Irritatingly, unless you can be sure that a cloth badge has been removed from an obviously original uniform it is very difficult to detect post-war fakes since the standards of manufacture are so high. The dramatic advances in computer-aided technology, allowing cutting, milling and die-stamping tools to be linked to mould etching or casting machines, are such that the problem of 'restrikes' is even more significant now than before. Traditionally, all that was needed to make a reasonably convincing replica was an original badge and some silicon rubber or plaster-based, mould-making materials. Once a cast had been made it was a relatively easy job to cast numerous replicas from a variety of molten (low-melt) alloys. Replicas passed off as originals are difficult to detect, even for the expert. There is no substitute for experience and collectors are advised to spend as much time as possible visiting museums and specialist collections to familiarize themselves with the correct appearance of original badges.

Many collectors are happy with copies, but the enthusiast Roy Smith sees this as a new and somewhat disappointing trend that can only serve to dilute the quality of the military insignia in circulation today: 'When I first started collecting, there were no reproduction insignia and the uniforms we sought were not for wear but to be displayed', he told us, 'Possibly I'm out of touch, but today the emphasis seems to be on re-enactment and original badges seem to be of little consequence.'

This lack of concern about authenticity has made it easier for reproductions to be passed off as originals and high production standards mean that it is often hard to detect fakes. The situation is exacerbated by the huge number of American insignia around, most of it possibly never worn in theatre. GIs could readily purchase replacement unit badges in their battalion PX; many simply collected examples of those of neighbouring units or purchased a variety of badges to be sent home to friends and family. American soldiers were permitted to own as many badges as they wanted, unlike the British squaddies' paltry 'Cloth, insignia, two'.

But collectors should note that American cloth insignia made in Britain while American troops were garrisoned here during the Second World War are of a quite different finish from those of American manufacture; thus it is easy to spot wartime originals. The essential difference between patches of American

Details of British regimental cap badges: Post Office Rifles, Buffs, Suffolk Regiment and East Yorkshire Regiment.

Canadian and Polish cloth insignia: Canadian national title worn before the introduction of individual unit titles or with titles that did not contain the word 'Canada.' Printed Canadian 1st Army patch, embroidered Black Watch of Canada (Royal Highland Regiment) shoulder title (the more unusual 'box' design format being used by units of the Canadian Second Division), embroidered Free Polish (2nd Corps) flash (this unit served in Italy during the Second World War); note the central figure representing 'The Mermaid of Warsaw' which features in local folklore.

Australian Women's Land Army woven cloth badge to be worn on milking overalls or housecoat, for instance.

and British manufacture is simple: American-made items are embroidered and those made under war economy conditions in Britain generally consist of overlaid pieces of cloth stitched together. It is more difficult to identify American officers' cap badges manufactured in Britain, just because thousands were held in stock in American quartermasters' stores over here.

Many American repro items are impossible to detect. During and following the war it was popular to collect American unit patches and to sew them on to blankets. In the USA dealers such as 'The Patch King' made insignia to the same high standards as those intended as government Issue. But generally, even today, British repro items are not made to such exacting standards and consequently are somewhat easier to detect.

But, as we have stressed throughout this book, there simply is no substitute for the actual scrutiny of genuine items, to determine exactly how the real thing is supposed to look, and the only really accessible place the average collector can go to see the genuine article is a museum. As a result, enthusiasts are urged to take pen and notebook to their nearest regimental museum or, in Britain, to one of the following: the National Army Museum (London), the RAF Museum (London and Cosford, in Shropshire), the Imperial War Museum (London, Manchester and Duxford), the Royal Naval Museum (Portsmouth) or the Fleet Air Arm Museum (based in Yeovilton).

Details of British regimental cap badges: Post Office Rifles, Buffs, Suffolk Regiment and East Yorkshire Regiment.

4 Headdress

The collecting of military headdress is a perennial favourite among enthusiasts. Nineteenth-century headdress is very rare and generally out of the reach of the average collector. The trend is now towards collecting twentieth-century caps and helmets and, ideally, examples of what may have been worn in combat. Increasingly today collectors opt for service berets too, not necessarily the elaborate French dinner-plate versions popularized by the famous *Chasseurs Alpines*, standard British army berets will do, especially as they come in a wide variety of types.

BRITISH

The colour of the beret usually shows what type of regiment the wearer was from. The range of British types available is surprisingly comprehensive, for example, khaki berets are worn by British foot guards; the Honourable Artillery Company and infantry regiments such as the Princess of Wales's Royal Regiment (formerly the Queen's, an amalgamation of many proud regiments including the Buffs, the Middlesex Regiment, the Royal Sussex and the West Kents); the Royal Anglian Regiment and the Green Howards. On the other hand, light grey berets are the choice of the Royal Scots Dragoon Guards, brown of the King's Royal Hussars and black of the Royal Tank Regiment. Rifle regiments wear dark green berets and include the Devonshire & Dorset Light Infantry, the Royal Gloucestershire, the Berks and Wilts Light Infantry, the Royal Green Jackets and the Royal Gurkha Rifles.

The choice available in British military berets does not stop with those indicated above. There are the maroon ones of the Parachute Regiment and the Special Air Service's beige version to collect. The Intelligence Corps wear a cypress green beret and

the Royal Military Police a scarlet version. Most other British army units wear navy blue berets, as do members of the Royal Marines and non-Commando-qualified Royal Marines (upon graduation Marines wear Commando-green coloured headgear). The Royal Air Force and the RAF Regiment naturally wear RAF blue-coloured berets. In fact, members of the Royal Tank Regiment, the Army Air Corps, Parachute Regiment and the SAS wear only their berets, shunning the peaked Cap No.1 Dress that appeared after the First World War, when the old scarlet jacket gave way to dark blue. The Cap No.1 dress is almost universally disliked by serving soldiers – hence its nickname of 'craphat'. The No.1 dress cap features a coloured cap band (red for all Royal regiments and corps) on which the regimental or corps badge is worn, a crown that may have coloured piping or a regimental or corps colour and a patent leather peak and chinstrap. Apart from the front of the cap receiving a stiffener in 1975 to make the profile of the cap above the peak almost vertical, it has remained nearly unchanged for almost a century.

One of the favoured collectables is the battlefield helmet. These are naturally robust and, unlike field service caps, unlikely to be attacked by parasites such as moths (however, we did have a particularly fine British Royal Engineers 'Arnhem' period para helmet in our collection the leather sweat band of which had been nibbled by mice).

Battlefield helmets are quite common. Being durable as soon as a generally acceptable design has been found – and we primarily have in mind classic American or Soviet patterns, the shells can be recycled and used by the armies of other countries; indeed, Egyptian troops sported Russian Second World War helmets at the time of the Six Days' War and, during the

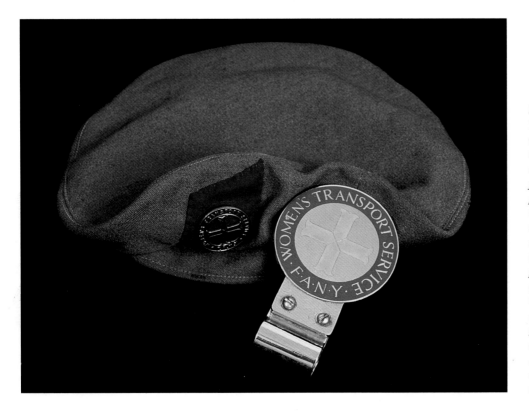

Second World War First Aid Nursing Yeomanry/Motor Transport Corps women's barathea beret with cap badge. The organization was created in 1907 as a first aid link between front-line fighting units and field hospitals. The cap originates from the beret/bonnets worn by the organization's motor ambulance drivers during the Great War. It has a value to collectors because the FANY was not supported by the War Office and was a quasi-private organization under the Office's umbrella. FANY essentially comprised women from 'the right background' who held driving licences. The badge is a standard bronzed FANY/MTC emblem with burgundy lozenge backing. A rare chromed vehicle mascot is also included in the photograph.

Example of a First World War British officer's soft trench cap. The officer pattern privately purchased seemed to retain a stiffened peak. This example is badged to the West Yorkshire Regiment and has a cap strap that has been split and braided; this was a popular non-conformist touch and was adopted by other ranks during the war.

First World War British other ranks' soft trench cap badged to a gunner in the RFA. Introduced in late 1916 to replaced the stiff service cap that could not be easily stored or carried when the then recently introduced steel helmet was worn. This example is made of woollen cloth although there are other versions made of a more drill type of material.

British Second World War vintage side caps: a glengarry of the Seaforth Highlanders worn by both British and Commonwealth-associated Scottish units, this pattern being most typical with its red, white and green dicing; officer's field service cap army in quality barathea cloth – a privately purchased item with both bronzed regimental insignia (Royal Artillery) and buttons; RAF ordinary airman's field service cap and brass badge introduced just before the Second World War and replacing the previous stiff service cap with patent leather peak.

LEFT: Khaki tam-o'-shanter or Balmoral bonnet. Introduced in 1915 and worn by Scottish troops during and after both World Wars, the example shown belonged to a Canadian Scottish unit, the Toronto Scottish. It is of Canadian manufacture, the badge backing is Atholl grey (the kilt of the London Scottish, the British regiment affiliated to the Toronto Scottish). All Commonwealth Scottish units were allied to a parent Scottish regiment.

Second World War British civil defence beret with cloth badge, a 'Basque' or 'schoolgirl'-style beret, of larger diameter and without the leather trimming of standard military versions, worn in conjunction with the civil defence battledress; but, because it is an ARP item, it probably predates the introduction of the complete uniform for civil defence services.

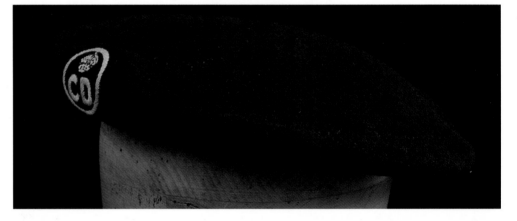

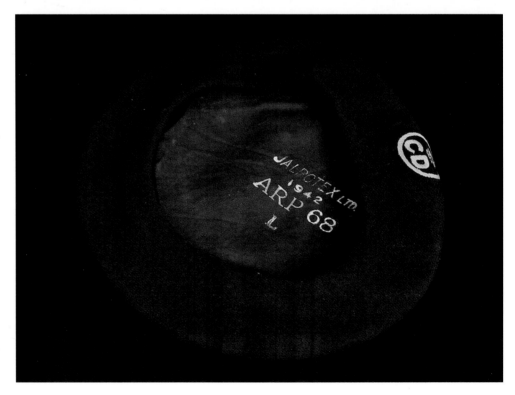

Interior of beret showing manufacturer, date, ARP stock number and size. Clearly marked and dated items command the highest prices.

RIGHT: *Interior view of British military Great War helmet, showing oilcloth cradle, felt top pad and leather 'pigskin' chinstrap. The bumper pads around the exterior can also be seen riveted through the top of the strap to which the liners are stitched. The helmet shell originally had a cover to the rim, now removed.*

BELOW LEFT: *British Mk II NFS green helmet with transfer, area number ('18') in the rim.*

ABOVE RIGHT: *British Great War military helmet with covered edge (effectively second production model), commonly referred to in collecting circles as a 'Brodie', after its inventor John L. Brodie who patented the design in 1915. Intended to be proof against 'shrapnel and falling objects', being pressed from a single sheet of steel, the new helmet was cheap and easy to produce.*

RIGHT: *Interior of the British military helmet illustrated above, showing details of liner and strap. Note manufacturer's code letters and numbers and steel batch numbers stamped into the rim.*

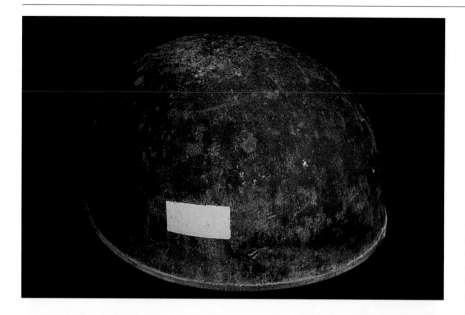

Parachutist helmet, 3rd pattern with webbing chinstrap, 1943 issue. The example shown belonged to either a Royal Signals paratrooper attached to airborne forces or a signaller who was part of a battalion of glider-borne troops. This helmet remained in service until replaced by the current Kevlar version in 1982.

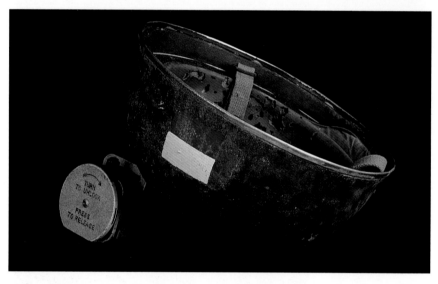

Interior of 1943 issue para helmet, showing complex liner construction. Collectors should note that this image illustrates the perils of neglecting protective storage: the previous owner stored the helmet in a rural area and rodents nibbled its leather sweatband. Next to the helmet is a surviving British parachute harness quick-release fitting.

British army khaki Second World War Mk II steel helmet. This went into production in 1938 to replace the First World War design. It resembled but is a completely different stamping from the previous model. The liner was altered and improved as well. Although at the time many First World War shells were refitted with new liners and strap mounts to be designated Mk 1*. Each liner could be more easily changed as it was screwed and not riveted to the shell, which, because liners were made in the complete range of hat sizes, was a necessary feature. Note the earlier spring-sided web chinstrap. This prevented injury should the helmet be lifted by blast.

ABOVE: French M1926 Pattern 'Adrian' steel helmet. This was an improvement on the classic First World War design, being a more robust, one-piece steel stamping. Interestingly, the famous French helmet was a first, named after its inventor Gen Adrian, a French officer fascinated to discover that one of his soldiers survived a rifle shot to the head because the Poilu wore his mess tin beneath his cloth kepi. Soon after, many other countries realized the protective value of steel helmets. The French employed a helmet-mounted system of identifying the branch of service. In this case the helmet belonged to the colonial infantry, native contingent troops drawn from countries from France's overseas possessions. Also shown is a French, Model 1931 military respirator, complete with haversack. In line with British and American fashion, French respirators featured a separate filter, attached to the mask by a length of hose and carried in the haversack, which, in turn, was slung over the head and secured around the body for added security. Two pockets inside the haversack contain metal tubes of decontamination ointment to be used only after a gas attack.

Indo-Pakistan conflict that followed Indian independence, both belligerents wore British-pattern Second World War shrapnel helmets.

AMERICAN

But overall, the most popular and copied design has to be the American Second World War M1 helmet. These may still be found relatively easily, but, as with all of them, their value resides in the quality and state of preservation of the helmet liner. This redefined shape, introduced in 1941 (replacing the First World War British design), addressed its predecessor's key deficiently — the lack of protection to the rear of the head and the neck area. When used on campaign in Europe, this helmet would be seen with a British-made net and chinstrap fastened across the rear.

ABOVE: Interior of French M26 helmet. The lining is of leather that hooks on to four mounting brackets fixed to the steel shell. Liners were sized individually, in centimetres, and could be easily exchanged to suit. Date and manufacturer's markings can often be seen on the interior face of these liners. It is common to find these helmets, part of the massive French reserve stock sold off by the government in the 1970s, without their unit insignia and with the addition of later, leatherette liners.

The American airborne helmet (M1-C) required only subtle modifications to the generic M1 army helmet and can therefore easily be faked. Often these were converted innocently for use by re-enactors, but, with the passing of time, have entered circulation as supposedly authentic '82nd Airborne helmets, as worn at Arnhem'.

The US Army tank crew helmet, once common, is now also harder to find. One of the reasons, of course has been the huge increase in 1:1 re-enactment, tankers' helmets being in great demand with the crews of American Second World War AFVs. Authentic examples are of lightweight composition and are essentially heavily padded crash helmets. Recognizing the often hot, unventilated conditions their crews would be expected to fight in, American designers pierced the helmet shell with numerous ventilation holes. When this helmet first appeared crews were expected to wear a fabric inner helmet, which featured a skirt to protect the neck. However, finding this uncomfortable, most crews wore under it either the US Army knitted cap, the equivalent of the British soldier's cap comforter or, another favourite, of American troops the woollen jeep or 'beanie' cap.

GERMAN

In terms of design, however, the German army's *Stahlhelm* has had the most influence. Protecting the lower neck – unlike the Tommy's battle-bowler, which was really proof against only falling shrapnel or debris, the 'Fritz'-pattern helmet shape now equips the troops of most modern armies. Most collectors of militaria aspire to owning an authentic Second World War German helmet, preferably in its original finish, like the example from

ABOVE: Second World War US MI infantry helmet. Designed in 1941 as a replacement for the British Commonwealth-issue helmet, the M1 was intended to offer better protection for the neck and the lower part of the head. In the war some 70,000 US troops were saved by wearing the helmet – this is especially impressive considering that the total killed numbered 368,000. In early versions of the helmet, the liner attachments or 'bales' were fixed direct to the helmet shell; on later versions, including those worn after D-Day, the attachments swivelled. Earlier liners were of a 'chunkier' composition. The key feature about the earlier, more collectable liners is that the internal straps (in either tan or green) were drawn together by a draw cord at the crown of the liner (rather than by interlacing) and that they featured a detachable nape strap at the rear of the helmet. After the war the allies extensively copied this classic American helmet lining, particularly Belgium which possessed thousands of surplus helmet shells. Thus it is often difficult to be sure of an actual wartime version. One tip for collectors is that Belgian versions sport the letters 'ABL' on the liner. But apart from this piece of evidence, many versions look authentic but are really post-war copies of the seemingly ubiquitous GI headgear. Worse still, the Dutch and the Danes stamped identical shells. The helmet shown features a British made 'net' because the equivalent American-made version did not arrive in theatre until late 1944 and too late for the second front. Consequently, until the American version arrived all GIs wore the same scrim netting as their British counterparts, even though this was made with the broader brimmed British helmet in mind.

ABOVE: Interior of a US MI infantry helmet showing the webbing head-cradle, part of the detachable liner (effectively a fibre helmet over which the steel shell fitted). The key features of the helmet were: the tan strapping, the way these straps were drawn by a cord at the crown, the small rear nape strap, the tan chinstrap and the leather liner strap passing over the front of the shell. Earlier MI helmet shells are identifiable by the non-flexible mounts that hold the chinstrap to the shell and the join in the separate rim being at the front.

US armed forces Vietnam-era steel helmet of 1960s vintage. It was a remodelled version of the classic M1, the basic shape and the liner harness assembly being modified. The helmet shown features a reversible (summer/autumn) 'frog leaf' camo cover with holes for mounting brush and an elastic retaining band into which a variety of items, including insect repellent, gun oil and even tooth brushes, could be fitted. As was usual during this war, conscripted GIs often customized the finish of individual helmets to express their individuality.

Very rare Nazi Allgemeine SS (Schutzstaffel) peaked cap. The more sinister of the Schutzstaffel branches (the other being the Waffen or armed SS), the black-clad members of the Allgemeine spread terror wherever they served.

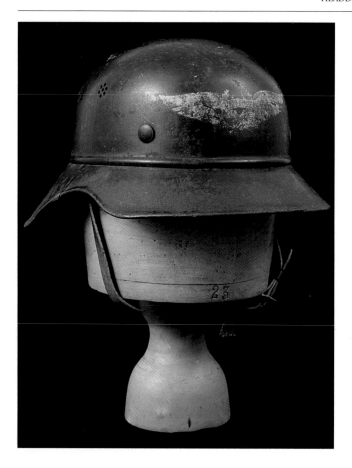

Second World War Luftwaffe (Luftschutz: air raid precautions service) helmet. A two-piece design different from the armed forces' helmets and of poorer quality. Across the front is a transfer of the insignia of the Luftschutz; constructed in sections for economy, German fire service helmets inspired its design. The use of lighter gauge steel than that employed in helmets for military service was another thrifty measure.

German Second World War M42 Stahlhelm; this version does not have the refined edge finishing of its predecessor (it has a non-rolled rim). The paint finish is referred to in collecting circles as 'Normandy' camouflage and follows that used on German military vehicles late in the war (sand background sprayed over with lines of green and brown).

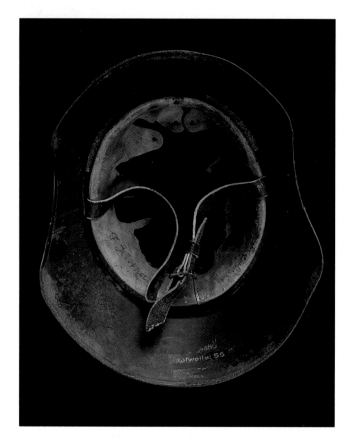

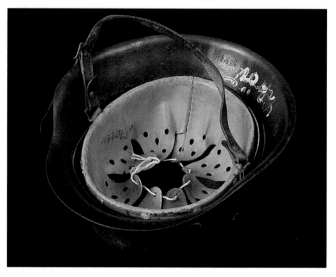

Interior of German Second World War armed forces helmet, showing leather cradle and chin strap. Shells and liners on this type of helmet were block sizes so that they would fit small, medium, large and extra large head sizes. At the rear, painted in white, are the soldier's name and number, a common practice. Visible too, stamped in the metal, is the manufacturer's coded identity mark. This helmet has no decals; after 1941 the German army applied only one. The single emblem denoted the branch of service, the army having done away with a decal of the national colours that provided a target (black, white and red – with a white stripe neatly in line with the occupant's temporal lobe). This helmet is in excellent condition, with the original finish with chinstrap and liner intact. As ever, originality is the key to value.

Interior of Luftshutz helmet showing leather cradle and strap.

Roy Smith's collection shown here. But with examples of the German Model 1916 version (especially the type converted to accept an additional 8mm armoured plate on the front to protect snipers) being the beyond the reach of most, collectors are forced to seek out its successor, the similarly shaped 1935 model. As might be imagined, these come in a wide variety of finishes – those with evidence of original decals reaching premium prices. Some German 1935 model helmets featured unusual turned-up brims; a very few issued to field signals troops and artillerymen featured cut-outs to allow the easy use of field telephones.

One of the most sought after German Second World War steel helmets is the paratroop's type (*Fallschirmjäger*). Although under the leadership of Kurt Student, Hitler had airborne troops as early as 1936, it was not until 1938 that these *Luftwaffe* soldiers possessed their own helmet. Its style was quickly copied by the British (as was the entire concept of parachute forces, something the Soviet Union had pioneered but which had largely been ignored by the British until Hitler used airborne forces to such deadly effect during his invasion of France and the Low Countries in 1940). To find these helmets is hard enough, but to find one complete with a camouflaged cover, introduced in 1941, is even harder.

CIVIL DEFENCE

In keeping with the current trend toward the collecting of items relating to the Home Front, both in Britain and abroad, there is increasing interest in civil defence helmets. Once wardens' helmets and those worn by British rescue crews or first aid parties were largely ignored. Often they were painted over in khaki by re-enactors to accompany the re-creation of Second World War

Second World War British civil defence Mk II helmet worn by a senior first aid party member identifiable by its colour, white and the two black stripes.

Black-finish factory firewatcher's helmet. It features the hand-painted badge of the Morris Motor Co.'s fire brigade.

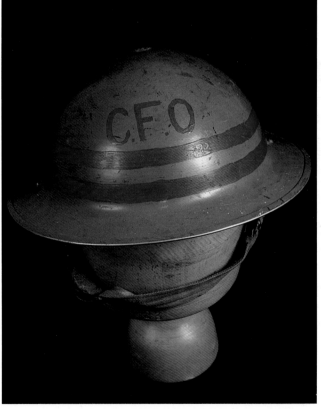

Green National Fire Service helmet with burgundy rank stripes and accompanying lettering identifying a chief fire officer, a more unusual format to the typical NFS helmet with NFS badge and area number transfers.

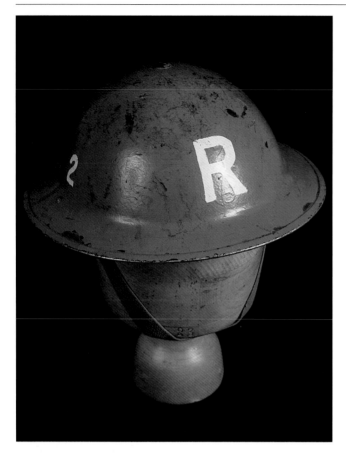

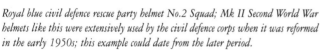

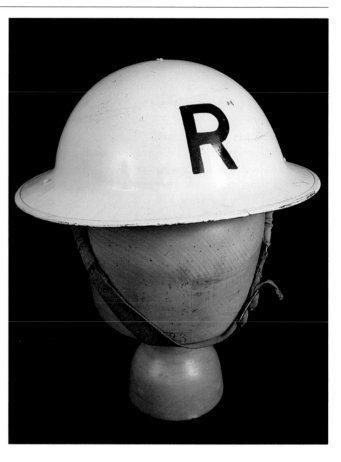

Royal blue civil defence rescue party helmet No.2 Squad; Mk II Second World War helmets like this were extensively used by the civil defence corps when it was reformed in the early 1950s; this example could date from the later period.

Mk II Second World War British helmet, civil defence rescue party leader in white finish.

Interesting example of a First World War British helmet recycled in the Second War and used by a clergyman working for the ARP.

A good example of a commercial British protective helmet. Produced to be marketed to private individuals or to certain groups and organizations prepared to purchase their own or to those who did not qualify for government ARP stocks.

Mk II Second World War British civil defence rescue party official; the white band denotes a team or section leader.

Mk II Second World War British civil defence rescue party member helmet. This has the variant of a smaller letter 'R' with the number '46' above either to identify the unit or possibly the individual.

LEFT: RAF leather 'C'-type flying helmet without earpieces or wiring loom. Shown with a pair of Mk 8 flying goggles and 'H'-type oxygen mask without hose. This helmet came into use in 1942, but the 'H'-type mask was manufactured from late 1944 and was not Second World War issue, consequently, the arrangement shown is more typical the late 1940s or Korean War period.

BELOW: British Second World War police helmet. The more common examples typically have the word 'POLICE' across its front, whereas this example has only the letter 'P'.

battledress. Today, even the most humble, rust-pitted civil defence helmet has value. Naturally, helmets with evidence of surviving stencilling achieve a higher price. One of the most desirable examples of the British civil defence helmet is the type fitted with an oiled canvas neck protector. Neck protectors were fitted to the helmets of rescue crews and wardens as a defence against the action of chemical agents such as mustard gas – the conviction of the time being that such attacks from the air were inevitable. Collectors should examine surviving examples of helmets fitted with such neck shields with care, and certainly before parting with hard-earned cash. As a result of being folded and stored for over half a century, these protectors are often 'sticky' and difficult to unravel. Furthermore, their oily composition often causes the rubber elements of chin straps and liners to perish.

As with all such things, availability dictates value. Before the fall of the Berlin Wall in 1989, East German *VoPo* (*Volkspolizei*) helmets, as worn by some army units and the *Vopo* Border Guard units, were fetching a premium price on the militaria market. Now, despite many of these classic Soviet designs' featuring fish-net camouflage netting and liner systems with chinstraps marked 'Made in East Germany', they are worth far less. When something is largely unobtainable it inevitably has value.

5 Uniforms

The twentieth century saw the real beginnings of practical, fully functioning uniforms for fighting men. The furious revolution in battlefield technology enabled killing with accuracy over greater ranges than ever before. Furthermore, the new weapons, both small arms and larger calibre field pieces, fired faster and could be reloaded with greater rapidity than previous models. Gone was the time when rival armies needed to stand out amid the smoke of battle so that their commanders could review the dispositions of their fighting men. Indeed, the advent of deadlier weapons, especially the machine gun, the power tool of the battlefield, made assembly in regular masses suicidal. The combination with mechanization meant that armies could suddenly and unexpectedly appear; speed, fire and movement were the order of the day.

AFTER THE FIRST WORLD WAR

After the Great War it was recognized that a new uniform, consistent with the modern battlefield, was needed. The British threw out the old-style service dress that, in one form or another,

had served its soldiers well, albeit since the Boer War in khaki rather than scarlet. However, it was not until 1939 and the start of the Second World War that this new battledress was ready. It is helpful to look at how this came about to illustrate the development of not just the British but also the combat uniforms of all twentieth-century armies.

The Boer War demonstrated to the British the need for stealth and concealment and the surgical precision of snipers heralded a return to temporary protective fieldworks; the German army adopted field grey for its uniforms, a colour that went some way to obscuring troops on the battlefield; and bright colours were no longer suitable for soldiers fighting a modern war. In Britain khaki was king; *khaki*, Urdu for 'dusty', allowed British infantrymen, armed with the new .303 Enfield SMLE, to pose a lethal threat on the battlefield; khaki uniforms were also easier to maintain than the scarlet tunics that preceded them. But British tunics were, however, still of the 'frock' kind, a type of jacket which dated back to the Crimean War and was still usable on the parade ground. Until the Second World War British uni-

Reconstruction showing First World War-period British infantrymen wearing khaki service dress uniforms with stiff and soft caps. The Highland soldier to the left wears the glengarry and a Gordon Highlander's kilt without cover. His tunic has the long, unpleated pockets and no shoulder 'rifle patches' of the 1914 economy tunic. The tunic front has been rounded to accommodate the sporran, a modification practised by both Highland and Lowland regiments. The soldier on the second left wears the divisional patch of the 34th Division. This form of cloth insignia for both divisions and battalions became a significant new feature of soldiers' dress as the war progressed.

Reconstruction of a First World War officer of the West Yorkshire Regiment. He is wearing the soft cap and tunic with second lieutenant's insignia on the cuff. By 1916 front-line field officers began to wear their rank insignia on their epaulettes in order to be less conspicuous. The officer depicted wears leather 'Sam Browne' field equipment, named after Gen Sir Samuel Browne (1824–1901). Legend has it that Browne designed the belt after his left arm was severed during fighting in India. The design is said to have helped to stabilize the belt so that the sword could be drawn with one hand. Details of 1908-pattern webbing equipment can be seen as worn by the two soldiers to the rear.

First pattern British army Second World War battledress blouse. Badged to a lieutenant colonel in the Worcestershire Home Guard. Note the unlined collar of the blouse and the plain khaki pips and crowns with coloured backing worn by the army early in the war and continued by the Home Guard thereafter. The medal ribbon denotes the 1939–45 Star. Introduced in 1943, this ribbon suggests that the officer had already seen some regular army service. Also shown with the blouse is this officer's khaki barathea and coloured field Service caps (Worcestershire Regiment).

forms, including the futuristic battledress that entered service in 1940, were made of wool – not the most practical material on a potentially wet field. This new battledress had a modern design and followed many of the principles established by students of the modern battlefield such as Liddell Hart and Fuller. It was also quite fashionable, the blouson and baggy pants combination was in keeping with the style of garment chosen by adventurers and skiers during the 1930s. It is often erroneously referred to as '1937 Pattern' but, in fact, it originated in 1938 but did not

enter service until 1939. One reason for the confusion perhaps is that the new web equipment designed for it dates from 1937 and is consequently known as '37 Pattern'. However, this revolutionary arrangement of belts, braces and pouches, designed to distribute weight across a soldier's upper body more evenly than the previous 1908 Pattern, as worn by in Flanders' fields was relatively complex to produce. Consequently, on the outbreak of war many soldiers wore the brand new battledress with the less satisfactory '08 pattern webbing.

British private soldier in late 1940 wearing 'unblancoed' 1937-pattern webbing and carrying a Mk V respirator haversack (worn at the alert). Across the top of his small pack his 'cape, anti-gas' is worn rolled. The bolt of his Lee-Enfield rifle is open and waiting for the magazine to be charged with two clips each of five rounds.

British soldier in early pattern battle-dress with respirator haversack at the 'alert'. He wears a Mk II helmet and carries his trusty .303 SMLE in the 'slung' position.

GERMAN

It must be agreed that the Third Reich introduced the first truly modern combat uniforms, made of practical materials and objectively camouflaged. In 1939–40 Hitler's *Algemeine SS* could don the *Zeltbahn*, individual ponchos which could be joined together to construct field tents and were printed with a disruptive pattern designed to blend in with the surroundings. The one advantage the Nazi party had when compared with the military regimes in other countries was that it was new. The election of Hitler and his party in 1933 swept away not only traditional military hierarchies it also condemned a great deal of existing military thinking as well. Certainly in Hitler's eyes such bourgeois principals had led to the stalemate and bloody frustration of trench warfare, he had witnessed it first-hand and was determined that his new army, largely built on bluff and histrionics to begin with, would be a modern force on the battlefield. *Blitzkrieg*, 'lightning war', which so nonplussed the allies from the invasion of Poland to the fall of France, was evidence of these new principles in practice. Just as the Third Reich threw away most of the outdated principals of its predecessors and adopted new theories to guide its armies in battle, it also developed a new system of dress designed to complement the pace demanded by the principles of *blitzkrieg*.

Even though Hitler's armies spent much of the war relying

Rare Wehrmacht *Second World War-period* Zeltbahn, *found in Normandy and a likely relic from the fighting surrounding the choked bridgehead. It is finished in what is referred to as 'splinter pattern' camouflage. Such use of camouflage and camouflaged patterned uniforms by German special forces was more innovative than that by allied forces. This clever garment doubled as a camouflaged, waterproof poncho and tent section, any number of which from three upwards could be linked to construct a bivouac. German soldiers carried pole sections to complete the construction of such tents, ideally assembled from four* Zeltbahn *sections. Additionally, by placing the head through a central hole, a camouflaged wrap-around cover can be formed for the individual soldier.*

Second World War German infantry lieutenant inspects an NCO and two private soldiers. All are dressed in early pattern, 1940–41-vintage uniforms. The private soldiers wear the Feldmutz *and their tunics are early pattern M36 models with dark green collars. All soldiers still wear jackboots, unlike troops later in the war, when ankle boots and gaiters were adopted instead. Also seen, representative of the* Blitzkreig *era, are cotton bags containing gas protective clothing attached to each respirator strap. Brown leather field equipment as worn by the officer is also typical of the early war period.*

on the horse as a prime mover for supplies and artillery and even though deficiencies of command would condemn hundreds of thousands of ill-equipped soldiers to a frozen death in Russia, on the whole, his designers provided the troops with a more practical uniform than that of other armies. Certainly, when compared to the often ill-fitting garb of British and Commonwealth soldiers, clad in the new 1939 battledress for which its designers had such high hopes, the *Wehrmacht* was in a different league as far as the fit and utility of their uniforms were concerned.

AIRBORNE FORCES

It could be argued that, irrespective of their function, German special forces, be they *Waffen SS* or *Fallschirmjäger*, pioneered some of the most advanced uniforms for their day. The allies watched German developments in military tactics and equipment closely. Indeed, Churchill encouraged the creation of a British parachute division after hearing accounts of the *Fallschirmjäger* breaching the Belgium fort at Eben-Emael, thought for long to be invulnerable.

German infantry officer, infantry NCO and artillery NCO of the Third Reich period. The artillery NCO is wearing the full-dress Waffenrock *with the red piping of his branch of service correspondingly seen on his service cap. He too holds the rank of Oberfeldwebel. Seen here are the 'Prussian' cuffs – two buttons surrounded by silver lace. The leather strap of the NCO service cap also can be seen in contrast to the silver braid of the officer. The letter 'G' in gold on the right sleeve of the figure on the left stands for Geschütz (self-propelled gun) and denotes a motor transport NCO (Schirmeister).*

German infantry Gefreiter (corporal) in greatcoat order equipped as he would have been in the early part of the Second World War. He is wearing the Feldmutz *side cap and belt order with triple leather ammunition pouches. Suspended from his webbing gasmask container strap is a grey-green cotton bag containing his gas protection clothing. The M35 helmet has on its left-hand side a decal representing the army eagle. On his back he wears a* Tornister *fur-backed pack and grey woollen bedroll. He is armed with a K98 rifle and around his neck carries machine-gun ammunition with disintegrating link for the MG34. Suspended from a coat button is a typical German-style torch with two coloured filters.*

German troops preparing a meal in the field using their mess tins and heating soup over an Esbit solid-fuel cooker. Note the two types of field cutlery – combined fork and spoon and clipped together knife, fork and spoon set. An authentic Bakelite fat dish is also shown and between the two cookers is the cup from a German army water bottle. Other noteworthy items shown include the fur Tornister back pack, the soldier's white collarless cotton shirt and the two white bands around the top of the soldiers' issue socks, which indicate their size (medium).

Thus the final significant development in uniforms of a kind familiar today was inspired by the requirements of special forces. However, after suffering loses amounting to 25 per cent when German airborne forces invaded Crete in 1941, Hitler not only decided that unsupported paratroopers offered little potential on the battlefield, a fact the Allies learnt to their cost three years later at Arnhem, he decreed that his *Fallschirmjäger* should wear camouflaged smocks. The British and Americans quickly followed suit and soon their airborne forces wore similarly designed and, in Britain's case, camouflaged jackets.

Essentially the idea of camouflage originated in Germany and the concept of practical combat uniforms in America. By the 1970s a combination of disruptive pattern material and cargo pants and smocks had been universally adopted as the ideal battlefield dress for fighting men. However, combat aside, the style and design of European and American 'best' – parade ground – uniforms, harked back before the Second World War to the first years of the twentieth century.

Although British airborne forces were themselves quite well equipped – certainly by the time of the ill-fated operation at Arnhem, when they were clad in state-of-the-art Dennison smocks – it was really American observers who had the next big influence on uniform design. With the introduction of capacious cargo pockets on combat trousers in 1942, American paratroopers introduced a further uniform change. Today, of course, combat or 'cargo' pants are taken for granted. Although British battledress trousers featured pockets, they were, in reality, of little use. German trousers, which, until the introduction of ankle boots, had to be capable of being tucked into knee-length 'jack boots', were even less generous.

MATERIAL CHANGES

German and US uniforms also brought about the next significant development in uniform design – the move to cotton and synthetics and away from wool. Interestingly, the Third Reich was forced by expedience, the lack of natural resources and dwindling imports, to adopt artificial materials. With the development of the then revolutionary material nylon – useful not just for stockings but as a replacement for the silk used in parachute canopies and which did not develop the static created by silk (which was found to be the major cause of 'Roman candle' fatalities) – the USA had discovered the most utilitarian of fabrics.

It is hardly surprising that traditionally, and certainly in re-enactment circles, enthusiasts have long preferred to wear German or American uniforms. The cotton or synthetic uniforms of both are not only easy to clean, they are also easy to reproduce, providing excellent bases for screen printing camouflage patterns and readily accepting of insignia such as cloth badges and patches. Furthermore, unlike the woollen battledress of British and Commonwealth troops, German and American uniforms were not susceptible to parasites such as moths or the dreaded 'woolly bear'.

Not surprisingly perhaps, given their popularity, by the mid 1990s stocks of German and even American Second World War military equipment were fast running out. While the repro industry geared itself to meet the needs of re-enactors and vehicle enthusiasts, British collectors began to select items of their own country's combat equipment. There was a surge in the collection of battledress blouses and trousers, enthusiasts being keen to configure a complete outfit, webbing then still being

plentiful. There had been a huge influx of brand-new battledress blouses in the 1980s when dealers took possession of the last surpluses from British army stores since the National Service days of the 1950s, but by the 1990s most of this was exhausted. In fact, other than those stocks, only officers' badged versions were still to be found; unlike soldiers and NCOs, officers owned their kit and were allowed to keep it when they left the colours.

Although Commonwealth battledress could be found, British collectors did not much like it. Apparently many re-enactors considered that the uniforms of Canadian, Australian and Indian troops related only to the war in the Far East, despite these nations' service in Europe. But one kind of battledress that was bought by British enthusiasts was that originating in Greece. Although of a slightly different finish from home-made uniforms and, of course, emblazoned with labels and stencilling bearing Greek script, for a long time many re-enactors were thus dressed. However, while supplies of original wartime battledress could still be obtained, the most prized possession was the special pattern of battledress trousers worn by airborne troops. These possessed large bellows front-leg pockets and two field-dressing pockets at the rear.

German infantry soldier's MG34 section c.1940 waiting by a canal. The one NCO and two private soldiers are wearing M36 tunics featuring dark green collars. The NCO is armed with an MP38 and on his belt carries the canvas pouches for its stick magazines. Noteworthy is the camouflage of the helmets, which use scraps of rubber or a bread-bag strap as bands into which foliage can be tucked.

OPPOSITE: *Picture shows German army officer of the Third Reich period wearing his dress tunic with full ceremonial accessories, silver wire and black dress belt with corresponding round buckle and silver wire braided lanyard. These uniforms were privately tailored for the individual. The white piping on his* Shirmutz *(peaked cap), shoulder boards and collar* Litzen *denotes that he is serving in the infantry. He held the rank of* Oberleutnant *as evidenced by the single star on flat silver board.*

ABOVE: *German Third Reich-period infantry NCO. This soldier held the rank of* Oberfeldwebel *(warrant officer). His tunic is the M1935 full dress* Waffenrock *for parade and walking out purposes. On the front left of the tunic the infantry assault badge is worn, denoting that he has taken part in combat. The German armed forces in both World Wars used this form of metal insignia to show either specialist qualification or combat experience.*

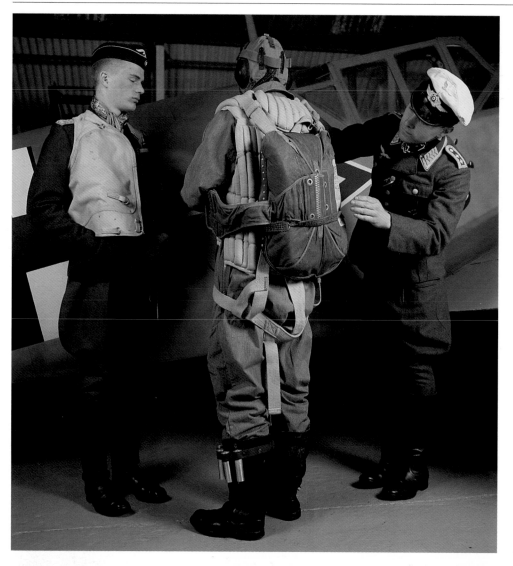

LEFT: *Three* Luftwaffe *aircrew members, including an officer and an NCO. In the centre a bomber crewman wears standard flying overalls, kapok life preserver, parachute and summer-finish flying helmet. To the left, the senior NCO (an observer) wears an other ranks' tunic (as opposed to the* Fliegerbluse*), breeches and cap with white summer cover. The officer on the right (an Oberstleutnant or lieutenant colonel) is wearing the* Fliegerbluse *and breeches in officer-quality cloth. He wears the corresponding officer-quality* Feldmutz *with silver wire piping and insignia. Interestingly the officer (a fighter pilot) wears the inflatable life jacket as worn by fighter crews. Note the flare cartridges strapped to the bomber crewman's boots.*

BELOW: *USAAF and RAF uniforms including the US B3 heavyweight flight jacket and trousers, Shearing fleece caps and boots. The officer is wearing one-piece green Army Air Force flying overalls, American aircrew parachute harness and a Mae West. The officer is in overalls and the other aircrew wear the famous 'A2' flight jackets.*

ABOVE: *Two ATS girls in ATS pattern battledress and leather Jerkins introduced during the mid war period,such change made necessary by the expansion of more physical roles for woman in the armed forces as the Second World War progressed. The sergeant closest is wearing a pair of sheepskin muffins devised for the ATS, which have a removable finger cover that allows precise work to be done without constantly removing the whole mitten.*

LEFT: *Member of the Royal Observer Corps with an OC marked British Mk II helmet, head set and chest microphone for telephone communication. It's early in the war because he's still in civilian clothes and only wears the OC brassard and enamel badge. Slung over his left shoulder is a military pattern respirator in haversack. Photographed at the Kent Battle of Britain Museum at Hawkinge, a front-line Fighter Command airfield in 1940.*

OPPOSITE: *Full-length depiction of a post-1942 Sussex Home Guardsman evocatively standing guard on Sussex Downland. He wears equipment that includes pouches and cross straps peculiar to the Home Guard, designed to carry the large magazines for the Browning automatic rifle (BAR). The Model 1903 'belt, Home Guard' is also featured. His water bottle is carried in a leather cradle with strap and his anklets are leather rather than the webbing variety used by the regular army. Over his right shoulder he carries a 'Lend-Lease' American P17 rifle.*

RIGHT: *Home Guardsman in early pattern denim battledress. He sports the brassard introduced when the LDV were renamed in autumn 1940. The Prime Minster felt that the nam Local Defence Volunteer was not stirring enough. Consequently, authentic items marked 'LDV', an organization that had only a short life, are rare. The soldier, wearing a khaki FS cap and carrying a slung military respirator, is armed with the Short Magazine Lee-Enfield (SMLE) a .303 calibre rifle. This famous and accurate weapon is fitted with a leather sling, which, like the rifle, was of Great War vintage.*

WHERE HAVE THE ORIGINALS GONE?

Nick Hall of Sabre Sales told us that there are some good reasons why re-enactors find it difficult to secure original battledress. First, he pointed out, most wartime soldiers were smaller than the more prosperous civilians of today. Often malnourished, being children of the depression, but now enlisted in a fighting force which made sure that calories were turned into muscle and not fat, Second World War infantrymen invariably had narrower chests and slimmer waists than today's re-enactors. The other reason for the post-war scarcity of battledress is perhaps less well known: much of wartime Britain was put to the plough to cultivate every available square inch of the countryside and civilians were encouraged to grow their own food and expand their allotments. The return of peace and the reviving import trade reduced the need for so much arable land; consequently, the authorities feared that the parts of Britain where the hedgerows and trees had been removed to increase yields might turn into dustbowls as unprotected topsoil was removed by erosion. With huge battledress surpluses, one of the most obvious products of

the peace dividend that came with demobilization, it was decided to shred most of it and use it to bind the newly fallow soil. According to Hall, there is one final reason for the post-war scarcity of battledress and this is no less fascinating than the others. Soon after the end of the war a plan was devised in Britain to feed people in the developing world displaced by the ravages of world war: the planting of groundnuts (peanuts) in Africa. To administer the scheme Dr Frank Sickling, an ex-RAMC officer involved in the development of hospitals, was chosen. However, the planners had not allowed sufficiently for the harsh African terrain, criss-crossed with thorn bushes and crawling with dangerous insects. Productivity soon dropped among the native contractors who were sunburned and developed infections. Hundreds of old Bren carriers and surplus turretless tanks were shipped to Africa in an effort to clear the terrain. However, Sickling realized that the suffering of the native workers had to be ameliorated and, in an effort to achieve this, surplus battledress trousers were shipped out in their thousands and used to protect the planters' legs from the sun.

Royal Naval personnel in Second World War rig as worn at sea. The duffle coats worn by the petty officer (left) and the rating (right) are described in the Navy as 'loan' clothing and belong to a ship's or shore establishment's stores. Under his tunic, the officer (a commander) in the centre is wearing the white roll neck wool jumper associated with the submarine service. The rating (centre right) wears traditional 'square rig', with white front shirt and blue jean collar. As was typical of British-based personnel in wartime, the headdress worn is 'black topped', white covers and ratings' hats for official summer being discontinued during the emergency. The ratings' cap tallies – HMS and HM Submarines follow wartime security procedures by not naming individual vessels.

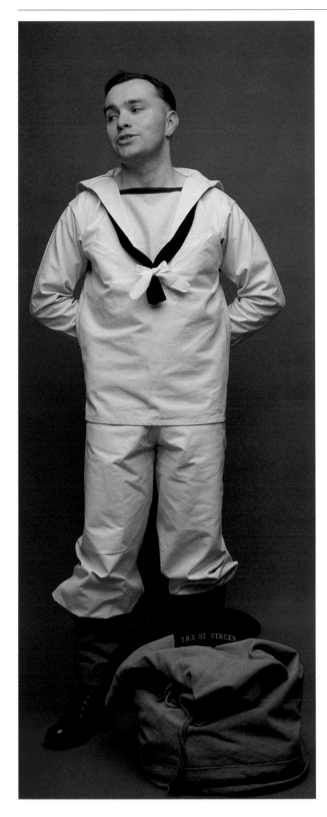

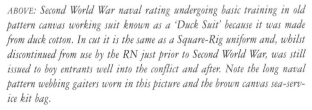

ABOVE: *Second World War naval rating undergoing basic training in old pattern canvas working suit known as a 'Duck Suit' because it was made from duck cotton. In cut it is the same as a Square-Rig uniform and, whilst discontinued from use by the RN just prior to Second World War, was still issued to boy entrants well into the conflict and after. Note the long naval pattern webbing gaiters worn in this picture and the brown canvas sea-service kit bag.*

RIGHT: *Holding a pair of Semaphore Signal Flags, this Second World War Naval Rating wears a white roll-necked pullover and black oilskin waterproof.*

Second World War navy gunnery rating at action stations. He is wearing a Mk II helmet, anti-flash hood and gloves, one-piece, blue, working overalls and money belt. His box respirator is of the long-hosed variety and therefore slung to his left side at the alert position with a special belt-type waistband securing the haversack to the body.

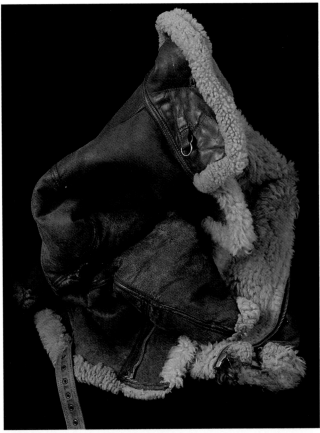

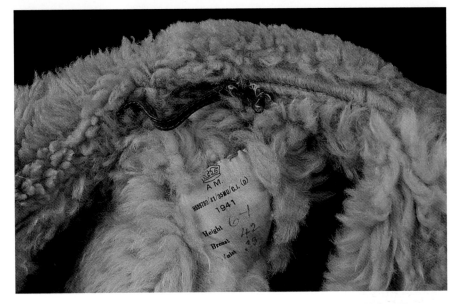

Irvine sheepskin flying jacket worn by RAF aircrew during the Second World War. Early versions came with symmetrical back panels while some later jackets were constructed from smaller, irregular off-cuts. Originally conceived as a suit with matching sheepskin trousers, of which there was an electrically heated version, the jacket alone is most typically thought of as being worn over service dress or even battledress by fighter pilots. There was even a version of the jacket, classified Coastal Command or Fleet Air Arm, that was complete with a hood, the rear of which was painted bright yellow to increase the visibility of downed crews as air-sea rescue units scoured the seas for them. This is a rare example of a classic piece of RAF flying equipment, dated 1941, with an obviously intact and original label giving stock number, date and size. Another point to look for to ensure authenticity is that the zip fastenings are marked 'AM' (Air Ministry). The Irvine is perhaps the iconic twentieth-century collectable.

One should mention here a little about the value added to those uniforms which display traces or 'shadowings' of previously applied insignia, such as a jacket showing the outline of *SS* runes or one that once featured an 82nd Airborne patch. Such links with the past can add real value if you can be sure of the history of a possibly otherwise unspectacular item of uniform. Certainly, for collectors, jackets with their insignia intact are worth a premium price, and combined they are worth more than the badges and battledress individually. A great many uniforms on the market have been 'doctored' by, perhaps, the addition of either real or reproduction insignia … buyer beware. Many enthusiasts, however, seem happy and such 'combos' are still highly collectable.

But one kind of uniform item hard to tamper with is the leather flying jacket. It is really not possible to disguise traces of needle holes in sheepskin or calf hide and so few try to remove insignia and pass something off with a spurious provenance. However, it is perfectly possible for emblems to be added to an otherwise nondescript item in an attempt to 'talk up' its value and purchasers of aeronautical items purporting to be of Great War vintage, such as RFC wrap-over service tunics (the characteristic 'maternity jacket') or the less iconic but still rare officers' khaki service tunic (RFC of army pattern) should beware. It is difficult to guarantee the authenticity of such pieces. Many items were privately purchased and made by bespoke tailors and, in any case, since the appearance of Howard Hughes's film *Hell's*

Three Battle of Britain period RAF pilots in a variety of iconic period outfits. These include an early pattern 'Sidcot' suit, officers' service dress and Irvine sheepskin flying jacket. Both Mae West life preservers are of the early pattern; one has been painted with high visibility yellow dope as used on RAF training aircraft such as Tiger Moths and Harvards. The officer in service dress wears the 'Luxor'-type goggles and the man in the Irvine jacket wears Mk III(a) goggles; 1936- and 1939-pattern leather flying boots are also shown. The flyer in the Sidcot suit has a seat-type parachute as worn by fighter pilots.

ABOVE: USAAF ground crewmen in a variety of woollen shirts, green herring-bone fatigue trousers, wool field trousers, A2 leather flying jackets and cotton field jacket. One ground crew-man is wearing the distinctive Army Air Force green fatigue cap.

RIGHT: Second World War USAAF bomber crewman in full flying rig. He is wears the B3 sheepskin flying jacket, leather flying helmet, B7 goggles and A10 oxygen mask. Also noteworthy is the first field dressing in rubberized cotton cover with two tie-tapes that attach to the harness of his Type AN6513-1A parachute.

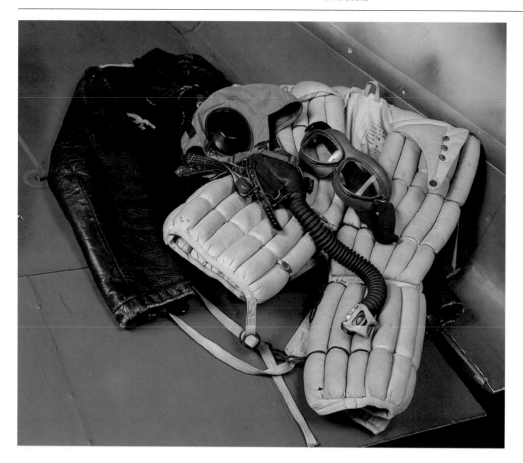

Luftwaffe *flying clothing:* kapok *life-jacket, canvas flying helmet, rubber oxygen mask with hose, flying goggles and the black leather blouson-style flying jacket which was often privately purchased.*

Angels in the 1920s many film costumes manufactured through techniques identical to those used during wartime have been absorbed into collections of genuine items. Faked Second World War items are easier to detect, the sheer effort involved in weathering and ageing reproduction Irvine flying jackets or *Luftwaffe* brown leather flight jackets being a major disincentive to fraudsters.

Collectors should closely examine American flying jackets, however. Many of the classic Second World War pilots' brown leather 'A.2' flying jackets have been enhanced by spurious painted insignia. Usually these colourful embellishments to the backs or the breast panels of these jackets bear the unimaginative legends 'Pursuit Squadron' or 'Flying Tigers'. Painted decoration can be quite easy to distress to suggest age, scuffs made with glass paper or by flexing to crack the surface finish often

being sufficient to suggest age. It is possible to find examples of surviving authentic flying equipment, and often what looks like the result of fraudulent meddling can be the genuine effect of long-term storage, for example, the authors' recently photographed consignment of quite rare, early pattern, one-piece Sidcot suits – the version with sheepskin collar and cuffs as worn by RAF crews during the Battle of Britain. The suits had been folded and stored for perhaps fifty years, they were intact, with perfect cotton twill finish and superb sheepskin detailing; their provenance could be confirmed, however, by one tell-tale piece of evidence: after years in cold and sometimes damp storage, the teeth of the suits' zip fasteners had partially corroded, leaving a criss-cross pattern of faint, rusty tracery etched into the fabric surfaces. Distressing of this kind is hard to fake.

6 Equipment

In the world of military collectables the term 'equipment' includes everything from the personal gear carried into battle by fighting men to the first aid kits carried by air raid wardens. It is also a catch-all for any large objects that do not readily fit into the categories of regalia, uniforms or ephemera.

SIZE NO OBJECT

As we have pointed out earlier, the selection of themes for collections is often determined by the amount of available storage or display space. Badges, the smallest kind of military collectable, are the easiest to amass in quantity. Even uniforms can be folded and packed away or sealed in airtight suit protectors and hung inside wardrobes, but it is not so easy to store a large number of Air Ministry bombsights or army field telephones. But, curiously, even though we are well into the twenty-first century, more examples of wartime hardware (principally from the Second World War and the conflicts in Indo-China) are collected now than were some twenty or thirty years ago, when they were a good deal closer in time to their origins. The explanation of the contemporary interest in military field equipment and civilian utility items is linked to the rise in re-enactments and displays involving vintage military vehicles.

Since the activities of the World War Two Battle Re-enactment Association (Second World War BRA) kick-started the organization of large-scale public events featuring vehicles and combat-dressed soldiery with the 'Battle of Molash' in the 1970s, mentioned earlier, there has been a huge upsurge in such outdoor activities.

Curiously, the recent upsurge in interest in full-size collectables, classic military vehicles, has encouraged a fusion of previously disparate collecting interests. Today's collectors of more esoteric field equipment, such as radios, may have started in the hobby while a radio ham or valve-radio enthusiast. Discovering that one source of these items is military auto-jumbles or re-enactment fairs often encourages an interest in the wider area of Second World War battlefield communications equipment and the pursuit of field radios, portable military telephone units as well as exchanges and even collectable cable drums. In 2004 the respected French publisher Heimdal produced *Les Matériels Radio de La Wehrmacht* (German Radio Sets 1935–45), so dealers can now expect a run on Torn.Fu.d2 sets, for example.

Larger objects of military equipment, being cumbersome to store, if not beyond the price range of the collector, are of most interest to re-enactment groups looking to enhance their

Reconstruction of a typical British air raid warden's post during the Second World War. Note the masked windows designed to prevent shards of loose glass from flying free should individual panes shatter. Also shown are a poster instructing the occupant on the identification of enemy aircraft, a range of official and commercially produced publications, a 'blackout lamp' (on the window sill – note the baffle preventing its beam from being seen from above), a gas alarm rattle and gas all-clear handbell and a fully equipped warden's first aid haversack. All these items are now highly collectable.

displays at public events. Now that much of the smaller, more accessible items of authentic wartime militaria such as badges and uniforms have been snapped up by enthusiasts, forcing novice collectors to be satisfied with 'honest' reproductions, about the only original items left are those larger pieces of field equipment that, before the growth of re-enactment events, no one wanted. Today, items such as cargo trailers, mine detectors, anti-aircraft mountings, artillery sights and field cookers are as eagerly sought as the RAF 'B'-type flying helmet and German *Stahlhelm* used to be.

The pages of the British magazines *Classic Military Vehicle*, *The Armourer* and *Skirmish* – the most popular publications for military vehicle enthusiasts, collectors of militaria and

re-enactors – testify to the increased interest in larger military collectables. The first periodical includes articles about past and forthcoming vehicle rallies and fascinating features on individual soft-skinned and armoured vehicles, and while one might expect to find advertisements for surplus jeeps, Land Rovers and even tanks, some of the other objects advertised make more surprising reading. Finding a tracked Volvo Snowcat Arctic warrior, a 1937-vintage *Wehrmacht* bicycle, a British cold-war MOBAT anti-tank gun and even a Great War-vintage United truck with a working, four-cylinder Wisconsin petrol engine – among many other and similarly rare items – is proof of the demand for such items. However, collectors on this scale need large gardens and even larger garages.

Contents of 1960s 'compo' ration menu D: as this covers a 24hr period, the contents are divided into breakfast, lunch and main meal. These are securely packed in tins and waterproof packing. Note the tactically non-reflective painted tins and brown, black-lettered wrapping. The energy content is carefully calculated, biscuit in ration packs substitutes for bread, tea with sugar, sweets, chocolate and sugary deserts not only provide energy but are also feel-good foods for men living under difficult conditions. Although dating from the 1960s, this pack is of an age to have some collectible interest. Such virtually nonexistent consumables are of considerable interest to collectors of Second World War ephemera.

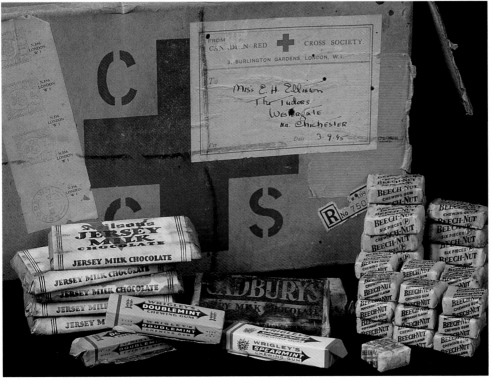

Chewing gum and chocolate bars.

Three housewife sewing kits and a pair of heavy wool OG socks.

Comforts and necessities including playing cards, books, spare laces, writing materials and handkerchief.

THE SMALL STUFF

Likewise *The Armourer*, jam-packed with articles about military uniforms and regalia, devotes space to the collecting of rather more cumbersome objects such as military water bottles, silver-plated Nazi teapots, British army rum jars and even inert ordnance, and then the re-enactors who comprise the readership of *Skirmish*, obviously satisfied with a good deal of reproduction material, use this publication as the marketplace for equipment such as entrenching tools, folding wire cutters and small packs. (But it should be remembered that a great deal of re-enactment focuses on conflicts in the Dark Ages, the mediaeval period, the English Civil War and numerous seventeenth and eighteenth-century battles, so there are also lots of articles about broadswords, mail and tricorne hats as well.)

With interest in the home-front activities of the warring nations seemingly ever on the increase, the collecting of civil defence items, and especially equipment used by Britain's Home Guard or the *Volkssturm*, the Third Reich's equivalent, is more popular than ever. For a long time items of webbing, the belts, pouches, packs and gaiters that, along with helmet and rifle, completed battledress, were commonplace and inexpensive. Now even they are in short supply. In fact, it is indicative of just how much was produced during wartime and perhaps of how long the war might have continued in the Far East if Japan had

Second World War German spade-type entrenching tool. This pattern of spade, with blade variants, was used by many European armies, both East and West during both World Wars. Around the tool are German munitions: rifle and machine-gun rounds, accompanied by a round egg grenade. The collecting of munitions, from small arms rounds to artillery shells and mortar bombs, is another popular sector of twentieth-century military collectibles.

First World War British tubular trench periscope dated 1917, War Office issue. This was carried and used in a more mobile context than the larger, boxed periscope permanently mounted on the fire-step of a trench. However, it has removable aperture covers secured to the body with string. At its base is a movable spigot with which to attach the periscope to the trench side.

First World War British soldier's D-type, two-piece mess tin, white cotton housewife sewing kit, home-made identity bracelet of a Royal Engineers sapper, set of later issue ID discs belonging to an RFA gunner (the secondary round disc would have been attached to a box respirator or its haversack after its introduction in late 1916).

First World War-period, steel-cased mirror with bracket for attaching it to a bayonet. On the end of the bayonet it could be angled so that it would be safe to look over a trench parapet.

British First World war trench observation mirror clipped to the 17in bayonet of a short magazine Lee-Enfield rifle to allow oblique observation of hostile terrain.

not succumbed to the atomic bomb that so much was produced. Nick Hall recalls that, soon after Second World War, a huge quantity of British webbing was burnt to release the brass fittings, valuable components and worth money if melted in quantity. He also remembered that he had been promised a huge number of quite rare maritime bicornes and other ceremonial helmets, long held in stock by the military outfitters Gieves & Hawkes. However, when he arrived to take possession he was dumbfounded to discover they had been burnt to release the precious metals used in decorating them.

It may be of interest for collectors to learn that they largely have the activities of Britain's Royal Navy to thank for the fact, despite recycling, so much authentic webbing has survived. Apparently, the Senior Service retained their huge stocks of 37

Pattern webbing until well into the 1990s. However, enthusiasts should note; it is generally estimated by professionals that there is no more than five years' stock of webbing left. So, if you are after such items, now is the time to purchase them; good quality, dated belts and bayonet frogs are even now becoming hard to find. The Holy Grail of the collector of British 37 Pattern webbing has to be the pouch specifically designed to carry two magazines for the Browning high-powered pistol – the automatic .45. (Remember that you saw it here first.)

ARP SURVIVAL KIT
Collectors of militaria, especially re-enactors, have long coveted original field dressing packs, but many enthusiasts have now realized the hitherto overlooked potential of ARP first aid

Exterior of an early make of rubberized cotton ARP first aid haversack supplied to local authorities.

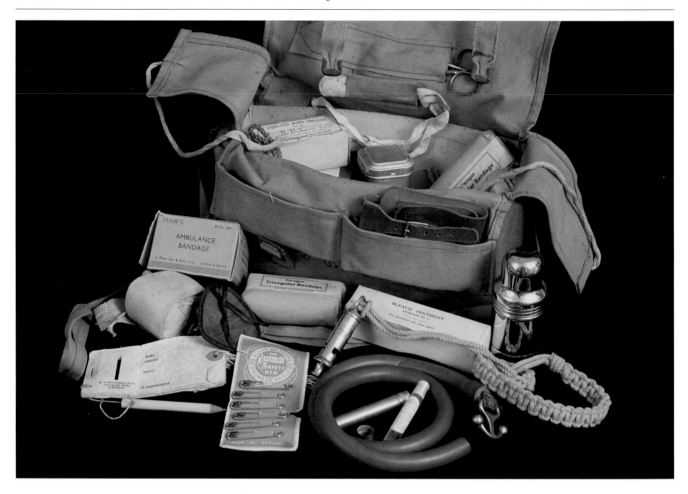

ABOVE: Contents of ARP first aid haversack including various sizes of dressings, tourniquets, eye patch, pills and ARP metropolitan whistle with yellow braided lanyard.

BELOW: 'Paragon' commercially-produced ARP first aid kit in rubberized cotton haversack. A good example of opportune marketing with contemporary first aid items – bandages, splints, lint and medicine glass packaged in a haversack marked 'ARP'.

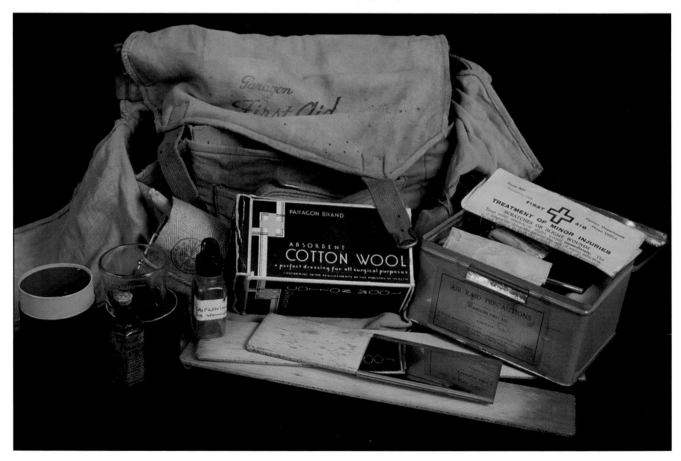

kits. These, usually packed in haversacks like the well-known Paragon brand are complete with a vast range of splints, tourniquets, ointments (often secured in delicate, glass-stoppered bottles contained in silvered cylinders), knives and scissors.

Complementing the survival aid equipment carried by wardens and rescue squads are the numerous respirators still available. Some, like the heavy-duty civil defence versions, came complete with microphones and earpieces to be worn by telephone operators during a gas attack. Children were encouraged to wear simpler masks, of the type dubbed 'Mickey Mouse' by virtue of the separate goggle 'eyes' and snout-like filter casing. Mint examples of standard British Second World War civilian respirators, complete in their original cardboard boxes (threaded with a length of string or held inside commercially manufactured

containers for wearing), with instructions printed inside the lid explaining how to pack, unpack and wear the respirator, are also worth keeping an eye out for. These previously commonplace items are now eagerly collected. Perhaps the most poignant examples of personal respirators are those designed for use by babies. The British version, a relatively large and cumbersome object, encased the whole child, leaving only the legs dangling free. The infant could be clearly seen through a large visor, rather similar to a space helmet. Being too young to draw filtered air in with its own lungs, the child's survival depended on the ability of the mother to continue to operate a concertina-shaped, rubber pump, which forced air into the sealed container. It was not clear what would have happened were the parent injured nor for how long she was expected to pump until the all-clear were

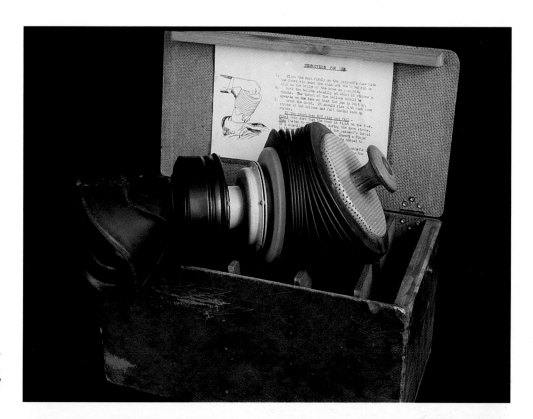

Second World War British home front-period, hand-pumped oxygen 'resuscitator' as used by first aid parties.

British Second World War civilian respirator with cardboard box and cotton covering case. Though these were produced in their millions and are still relatively common, they are difficult to find and maintain in good condition, the thin black rubber of the edge of the face piece being subject to deterioration, becoming dry and brittle.

Two British Second World War respirators specifically designed for babies. These rather fearful looking devices were quite well designed, covering the baby within a protective cocoon and offering some protection from debris. Its one shortcoming was the necessity for the mother to continue to operate the concertina bellows pumping air into the compartment containing the infant. If the adult were incapacitated the baby would have quickly perished. Also shown in the photograph is the official Home Office Air Raid Precaution Department's publication Anti-gas protection of babies and young children. Some Second World War nurses' headpieces and disposable bibs are also shown.

British military-pattern 'box' respirator from the Second World War carried by essential civilian personnel on the home front such as policeman. The haversack still bears traces of the words 'Remote breathing apparatus' because this model enabled rescue crews to implement a 'buddy', shared-breathing system, similar to that used in scuba diving.

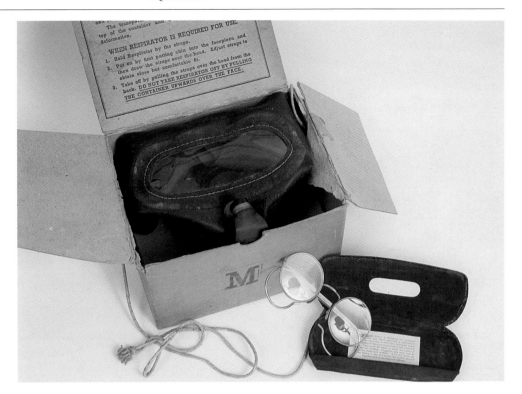

Second World War British civilian respirator in its cardboard box showing care instructions on the reverse of the lid. The letter 'M' on the front of the box indicates that it is a medium-sized mask. This particular mask is a slightly different and more unusual version, having a black surround/seal to the mica eyepiece. Also, like the civilian duty respirator, the mask has a flutter valve exit hole above the filter. Next to the box are a pair of military respirator spectacles and their case. These have 'arms' made from flexible steel strip that fitted snugly under the mask.

sounded. Interestingly, surviving examples of German infants' respirators from the Second World War can still be obtained. As one might expect from a nation with a proud tradition for practical engineering, the German solution was ingenious, if not a little impersonal. Once secured within its gas-tight container, the child was supplied with air by the simple expedient of the mother's operating a foot pump. Thus the baby could be suspended from a suitable hook while the mother continued to read or sew.

British ARP 'gas rattles' have, like gas masks and even the most nondescript civil defence helmet, achieved desirability in recent years. Collectors should carefully study any rattles passed off as those used by wardens. Commercially-produced football rattles were available in their thousands pre-war and, to be fair,

ABOVE: Second World War British air raid warden's whistle and chain. Manufactured in Birmingham and clearly marked 'A.R.P.', when this whistle was blown its sound was often followed by the barked instruction to 'Put that light out!'

RIGHT: Two pieces of early ARP equipment: a wooden rattle and brass bell. Both were to be used in the event of an aerial gas attack. The rattle to signify 'Gas!' and the handbell the 'All clear'. Both are ARP-marked and may have been manufactured before the Second World War, possibly at the time of the Munich Crisis in 1938. Clearly marked items like these naturally command the highest prices.

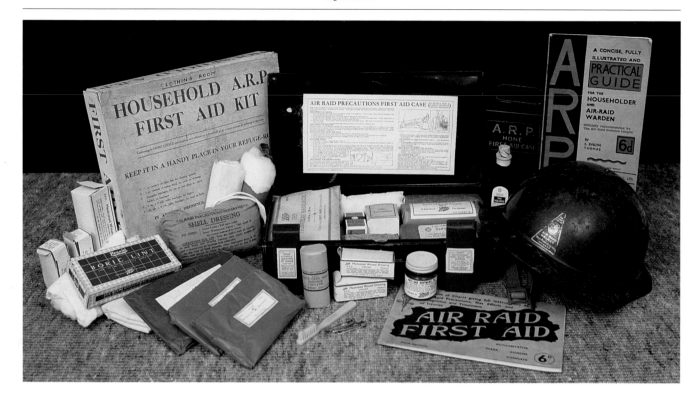

An arrangement of household ARP items including two examples of the 'Boots A.R.P. Home First Aid Case' and contents; a Home Office-approved 'Household A.R.P. First Aid Kit' ('Conforming to Home Office specifications and sufficient for a household of six to seven persons all sheltering in one room'); a privately purchased air raid helmet, manufactured by Head Protectors Ltd of Grimsby, and a selection of period instructional pamphlets.

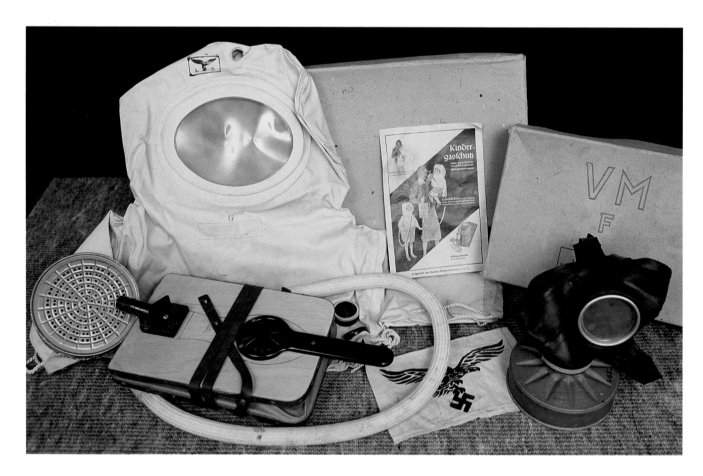

A selection of German Second World War Luftschutz (ARP) items. In the picture from the left is a particularly rare mint and boxed German babies' respirator (notice the Luftschutz emblem printed above the visor and the surviving instructional leaflet showing the equipment in operation); a Luftschutz armband to be worn in conjunction with the helmet shown on page 46 and a civilian respirator.

ABOVE: *Collection of Second World War German airman's papers, including his identity 'Soldbuch', calendar for 1943, chart of military map symbols and letter. Most probably collected from a POW or casualty at the end of the campaign in North Africa.*

RIGHT: *A rare find, this is a small section of a large (8ft ¥ 6ft) German Operation Seelöwe invasion map from 1940. The map shows the likely invasion areas of Kent and Sussex; the map is an overprinted version of a British Ordnance Survey map – the Germans not caring for the niceties of copyright infringement.*

many used by ARP members started life on the terraces. However, official ARP-stamped rattles can be found and are naturally more valuable. Rattles were intended to signify a chemical attack. To distinguish the all-clear when a raid had passed and the poison dissipated, brass hand bells were used. As with rattles, often commercially-produced bells, as used by schoolteachers and town criers, were often pressed into service. However, examples stamped with ARP insignia can still be found, but at a premium price.

AIRCREW EQUIPMENT

Perhaps one area where the collecting of equipment, rather than of insignia or combat clothing, is seriously pursued is in aircrew equipment. For British collectors of RAF equipment the most sought-after items include the 'B'-type leather flying helmet of Battle of Britain vintage, mentioned already. This helmet is easily identifiable by the two zip-fastened leather blisters enclosing the earphones. To accompany this helmet most collectors also seek a pair of Mk IV goggles. These featured flip-down

Recognition models, used to train the Home Guard and civil defence forces, notably the Observer Corps, to tell the difference between friend and foe; these can still be found in junk shops or at car boot sales. This lovely Spitfire is moulded in one of the very early cellulose plastics. This material is quite fugitive and prone to fatigue and warping. Although this model has lost a tail plane, it is still in remarkable condition considering its age.

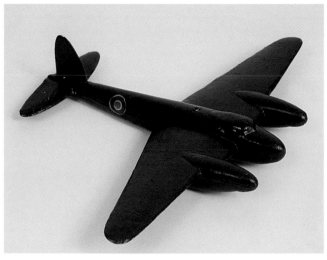

This recognition model of a Mosquito fighter-bomber is made of paper. Very fragile, this miniature (made to the 1/72nd scale pioneered by James Hay Stevens's pre-war Skybirds models) still bears traces of its original decals.

polarized sun visors that could be employed when the wearer was attacked by 'the Hun in the sun'. To complete the perfect early flying helmet combination, a type 'D' oxygen mask/microphone attachment should be added, but this is the most desirable piece of British flying equipment and most collectors are forced to opt for a reproduction version. But it is still possible to find examples of the RAF's type 'C' helmet. This was introduced in 1941 and did sterling service well into the 1950s. Although well made in leather, the rubber cups protruding from the earpieces can easily identify it; these were used to secure headphones. The rubber type 'G' oxygen mask accompanied the type 'C'. Pilots generally opted for the classic Mk VII, leather-padded goggles of the type also worn by most motorcyclists in the 1950s and early 1960s. Original Second World War RAF 'Mae West' life preservers and complete parachute and harness assemblies can rarely be found outside museums. The originals were always returned to depot storage and the life preservers embodied many perishable rubber components and so few complete examples survived in any case.

As with RAF gear, *Luftwaffe* flying helmets are probably the most sought after pieces. The basic helmet came in two versions: a lightweight, canvas one for use in summer (worn by many crews during the Battle of Britain, of course) and a heavier version made from leather and similar to the RAF equivalent. The

earphone fixtures on *Luftwaffe* helmets were quite different, however, the earphones being secured in slim, moulded enclosures. Luftwaffe microphones were also quite different; unlike the RAF's solution, they were remote from oxygen masks, consisting instead of discreet throat models incorporated in the helmet's neck strap. Ideally, collectors of *Luftwaffe* flying equipment should posses a pair of the classic shatter-proof, Nitsche und Gunther goggles; but prospective purchasers of these large, one-piece goggles should carefully examine the rubber surrounds of the eyepieces; because of their age, it is very likely that the light coloured material will have partly perished.

Whereas British and allied life preservers were inflated and could, consequently, be punctured, early *Luftwaffe* versions were far simpler. The classic *Luftwaffe* version worn during the Battle of Britain period consisted of sausage-like lengths of material filled with kapok. Again, these are likely to be found only in museums; some of the finest examples in Britain are in the Battle of Britain Museum at Hawkinge in Kent. There is a huge amount of very collectable Battle of Britain-period flying equipment at Hawkinge, both RAF and *Luftwaffe*; this is fitting because, as many readers will know, RAF Hawkinge was a front-line airfield during 1940, it was situated inland high above the cliffs and a stone's throw from the area dubbed 'Hell's Corner'.

7 Weapons

In the United Kingdom, until around twenty years ago, it was not possible to collect twentieth-century military firearms legally other than service rifles that had been smooth-bored so that they were classified as shotguns and kept on shotgun certificates. Apart from a few re-enactors who had applied for and been granted a firearms certificate, the possession of the classic service rifles was beyond the scope of most collectors.

THE SHARP END

It was only with the official acceptance of certificated deactivation that enthusiasts were able to own non-firing examples of everything from military handguns, rifles and automatic machine-pistols, to heavy machine-guns and even mortars. Coincidentally at around this time, there were still large stocks of Second World War-vintage weapons in ordnance reserves and government stores – especially in Australia and other Commonwealth countries. As their arsenals were redeveloped, many of these nations earned considerable foreign exchange by selling obsolete weapons, many of which had been coated in grease and packed away since the Great War. As a result of these weapons being made available, the market was awash with British weapons, the trusty .303 Lee-Enfield being particularly common. Some of these recently deactivated weapons were models that were, in fact, obsolete by the time of the Second World

War. Consequently, such items as the .445 Webley pistol, Lee-Metford rifle and the Lewis gun commanded sky-high prices. Of these, the Lewis gun is perhaps the rarest and most coveted. It is assumed that, with the introduction of the Bren gun in the late 1930s, most of the existing Lewis guns were scrapped. However, as every military enthusiast knows, this and the perhaps the more famous Vickers machine gun played key parts in the unfolding story of British firearms in the twentieth century.

Until the arrival of deactivated original weapons, collectors and re-enactors without firearms certificates had to make do with full-scale replica weapons of the kinds that were imported from the Far East and enormously popular with enthusiasts in the 1970s. At this time many a weapons mount on a classic military vehicles carried an Asian facsimile of a real weapon, and very good many of them were too. However, since the first wave of legislation restricting the ownership of certain deactivated weapons came into force in the 1990s, a natural reaction to the outrages perpetrated by crazed gun men even in Britain and the laws of supply and demand have greatly affected the values of deactivated display weapons. The original legislation principally effected semi-automatic rifles and sub-machine guns, prohibiting the inclusion of 'moving parts' in the breeches of these weapons which allowed them to be cocked. As a result, prices for the dwindling supply of the weapons sold and certificated before the introduction of the new rules have jumped, American M.1

Bren light machine gun being operated by members of the Royal Sussex Regiment. When first developed, the Bren was found to be too accurate. Consequently, it was re-engineered to produce the wider spread of bullets more useful as an area weapon on the battlefield. A two-man team in each infantry section would operate one Bren gun. Firing a compatible .303 round, its design was, in effect, the catalyst for the 37 Pattern webbing. Its high rate of fire meant that each soldier within a section

was required to carry two spare magazines to service the weapon – hence 'Bren pouches'. These new pouches also addressed the deficiencies of the previous Model 1908 equipment that had only pockets for clips of Lee-Enfield rifle rounds. Now a soldier could carry his own bandoliers of rifle ammunition and also have space for grenades and the other evolving section weapons: the Boys AT rifle, but principally the 2in mortar.

The Bren Light Machine Gun – Description, Use and Mechanism, *Second World War booklet published by Gale & Polden. This classic British weapon was based on the Czech ZB 26 MG and transformed into the Bren by Enfield's Royal Small Arms Factory in 1937.*

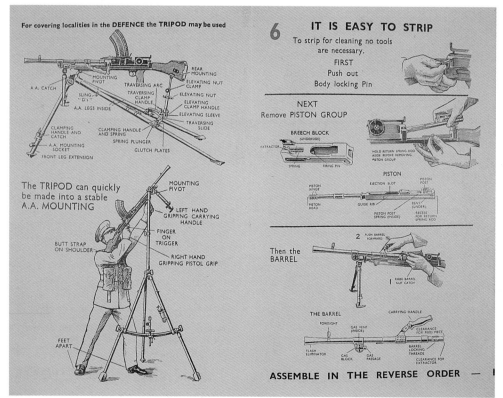

Pages from Gale & Polden's guide to the Bren gun, showing how the weapon's tripod could be combined with an anti-aircraft mounting and how easy it was to strip and clean the weapon without the need for tools. Generations of wartime soldiers and the thousands of National Servicemen who followed them learnt to perform the operations shown in their sleep.

Garrand rifles and German MP40 sub-machine guns more than trebling in value in less than a decade.

Some weapons, such as the famous British Martini-Henry rifle from the later part of the nineteenth century, are exempt, the government presumably thinking that few would attempt to hold up a bank with a weapon most people see on television every Christmas when *Zulu* is screened. But the reason these weapons have been spared is that, being of an obsolete calibre, ammunition for functioning versions of these weapons would be nigh on impossible to find. Furthermore, many 'modern' bolt-action rifles, such as the Lee-Metford and even the Lee-Enfield, are now over 100 years old and eligible for classification as antiques.

However, for the first time, to classify a weapon as an antique or as a firearm simply by virtue of its age will no longer be relevant. Very soon many prohibited, semi-automatic weapons and machine pistols, as, for example, the German army's first sub-machine gun, the *Bergmann MP 18.1*, a 9mm weapon introduced by the Central Powers in 1918, will fall into the classification 'antique' yet it possesses a mechanism explicitly banned by current firearms legislation.

THE LONG ARM OF THE LAW

At the time of writing (2006), collectors and especially re-enactors, have been concerned about further changes in British law concerning the sale and ownership of antique firearms. This is understandable given the rise in firearms abuse, since the possession of functioning pistols, rifles and automatic weapons has long been restricted and, as we know, even modern deactivated pistols or deactivated automatic weapons with partially working mechanisms are prohibited too. But there is a real concern that things might be tightened up even further, preventing re-enactors from mustering in the fullest combat equipment. A recently-published Crime Survey shows that government intervention has resulted in a reduction in violent crime of an impressive 34 per cent, so it is hard to argue with many of the new measures.

However, military enthusiasts owning muzzle-loading flint and wheel locks or percussion-firing antiques, and especially

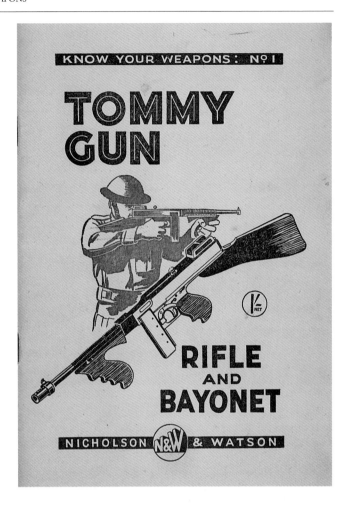

RIGHT: Know Your Weapons, No.1, *by Nicholson & Watson. Describing the Tommy gun (Thompson sub-machine gun), an American weapon issued to Special Forces and the Home Guard and famously popularized by the Prime Minister Winston Churchill (whom the Nazis likened to a Chicago gangster).*

BELOW: A Second World War chart for the .300 Lewis gun of the sort stuck to the bedroom walls of countless British schoolboys. The Lewis gun was produced in two calibres, .300 and .303 (which was compatible with standard British cartridges). Immediately following the evacuation from Dunkirk, where most of Britain's equipment was left behind, a large quantity of Lewis guns were purchased from the USA. However, most of these ended up being used by the Home Guard and the merchant marine.

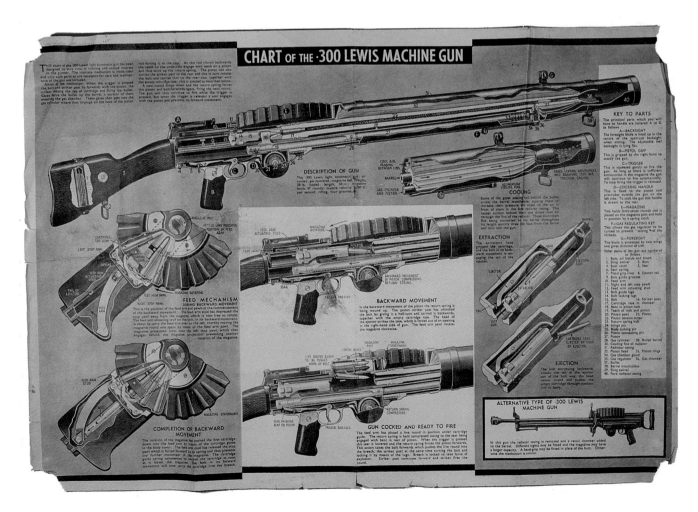

Two members of the Home Guard train in denim battledress with their Boys anti-tank rifle. Although this 0.55in weapon had a fearful kick, it was largely obsolete before the war started and was superseded by the Projector Infantry Anti-Tank (PIAT), a type of bazooka, when this weapon was introduced later in the war. Operators of the Boys were encouraged to aim for the weak spots of German Panzer

I and II tanks (really the only German tanks this weapon was capable of damaging in any way). Consequently, British crews were told to shoot at the tracks, vision slots and the join between the hull and the turret or, if they were lucky and the enemy AFV was on a ridge and exposing its belly, the thin armour of the vehicle's underside before it tipped downwards.

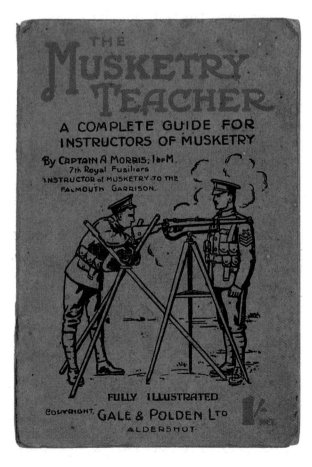

British manual of musketry dating from the Great War published commercially by the well-known firm of Gale & Polden. Such publications were designed to cash in on the enthusiasm of patriotic volunteers to 'do their bit' in wartime, the distribution of official War Office manuals being more tightly controlled.

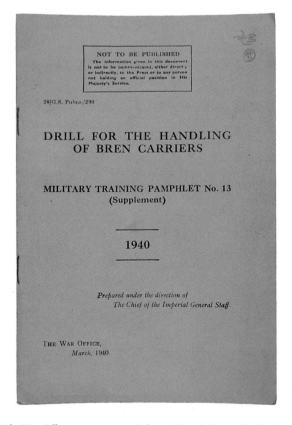

British War Office training manual from 1940 dealing with the Bren or 'Universal' carrier. There exists an enormous range of similar publications for British, Commonwealth and American forces, dealing with everything from in-depth technical notes to battlefield tactics, field craft, intelligence briefings about enemy forces and equipment, to copious stores lists. These are mostly easily come by and thus relatively inexpensive, but they do provide a mine of information to the enthusiast.

those collectors of previously deactivated weapons, have been in a quandary about the legal status of their collections. During a debate in the House of Lords on 26 March 2006, Baroness Scotland of Asthal, Minister of State in the Home Office, recommended that the Violent Crime Reduction Bill be returned with amendments to the Commons for the second time, saying:

> The definition [in the Bill] specifically excludes deactivated firearms and imitations of antiques, as well as any imitations which are antiques in their own right. I know that some collectors of real antique firearms are concerned that we have used 1870 as a reference point when there is no fixed date for antiques in the firearms acts. I should explain that this date was chosen because it was only after then that the manufacture of a particular type of breech-loading firearm became widespread. I am happy to put on the record that we see this date as having relevance only to the Violent Crime Reduction Bill; it has no effect on the provisions of the Firearms Act 1968 which deal with the status of real antique firearms.

It is assumed that re-enactors and collectors who have long had to abide by the provisions of the 1968 Act will experience little change in the pursuit of their hobby. Indeed, on an official British police website (the Devon and Cornwall Constabulary) the authors found the following under the heading 'Buying deactivated weapons': 'It is important that care is taken when acquiring any firearm that is described as deactivated. You should ensure that you are shown the proof house mark and certificate issued in respect of any gun deactivated in the UK since 1989.'

Nevertheless, it must be admitted that the prolonged uncertainties relating to the status of deactivated weapons have encouraged many enthusiasts to dispose of their collections and many dealers to cease trading in them. Because of the confusion regarding the legality of buying and selling such unusable weapons their value has also dropped significantly.

WEAPONS AND ARCHAEOLOGY

One more recent feature that is part of the hobby of collecting vintage weapons relates to firearms that will never be used offensively. This involves what enthusiasts consider a valid part of battlefield archaeology and sceptics consider is digging for scrap – unearthing rusty relics from fields and the foundations of building developments. The trade in such excavated ordnance has also stimulated the interests of local authorities, both here and abroad, concerned that, sooner or later, an amateur military historian will disturb a cache of live explosives and trigger a disaster. However, despite the bureaucratic and health and safety hazards encountered when professional historians such as Richard Holmes or Brian Knight unearth the corroded firing mechanisms of weapons, they often reveal details which add to

Improvised 'butterfly bomb', manufactured as a training aid for Home Guard and civil defence purposes. This German Second World War anti-personnel device was used against British civilian targets and on the battlefield. In essence it was the forerunner of the modern cluster bomb. Numerous such 'bomblets' were dropped, their descent being retarded by the spring-loaded 'sycamore leaves'. This prevented the bomb from detonating on impact, allowing it to remain, armed and ready to explode if tampered with. Frequently caught on overhead cables or telegraph lines, these deadly munitions proved difficult to clear and were a time-consuming irritant to engineers and bomb disposal teams. There are accounts of them being painted with bright yellow bands to encourage children or animals to interfere with them to deadly effect.

Second World War German incendiary – the notoriously effective 'Firebomb Fritz'. Designed to be dropped in large quantities over urban areas to create uncontrollable firestorms, they detonated on impact, igniting a magnesium compound that rapidly burned white hot and was difficult to extinguish. Notorious for their habit of crashing through roof tiles and setting fire to timber joists, not all of them detonated, 'duds', often without their delicate aluminium tailfins, became sought after schoolboy souvenirs.

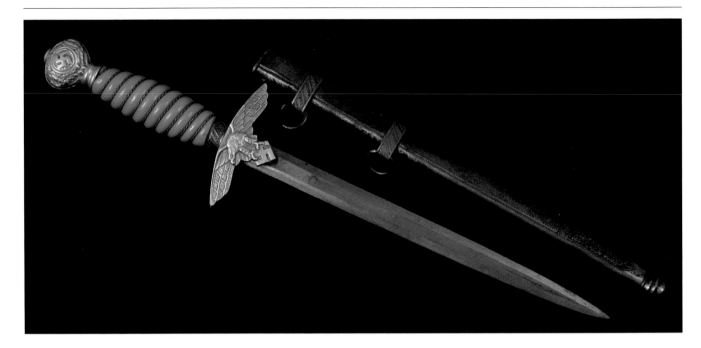

Third Reich Luftwaffe *officer's dagger. From members of the military and the party to administrators in the railways and even forestry officials, the Nazi state introduced daggers for every conceivable organization. They were designed as a symbolic representation of a badge of office. Together with Nazi insignia and headdress, these items probably rank among the first Second World War souvenirs to be collected, being much prized by allied servicemen who eagerly 'liberated' them from their owners. Being such highly prized battlefield souvenirs, not surprisingly, they were heavily copied in a surprising range of quality finishes. Surviving daggers often have missing or replaced pommels, hilts and handles, so the collector has to be vigilant. As always, value is dictated by condition, the highest prices being commanded by examples with their hangers and knot intact.*

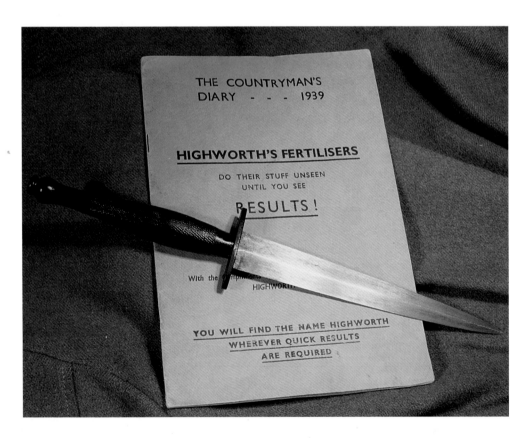

Fairbairn-Sykes fighting knife. A typical wartime example with cross-hatched handle but without the Wilkinson Sword logo etched on to the blade. Closely associated with commandos or airborne forces, the example shown is an authentic weapon as issued to a member of the fabled Auxiliary Units. This knife belonged to Auxilier Geoffrey Bradford; it is shown adjacent to his own copy of The Countryman's Diary 1939, *this rather innocuous looking pamphlet was a handbook for murder and mayhem, instructing Auxunit members about the finer arts of assassination, explosives and concealment. The legend, 'Highworth's Fertilisers Do Their Stuff Unseen Until You See Results!' alludes to the document's lethal intent – Auxunit volunteers learned their dark arts at Coleshill House, a country house near the Wiltshire village of Highworth.*

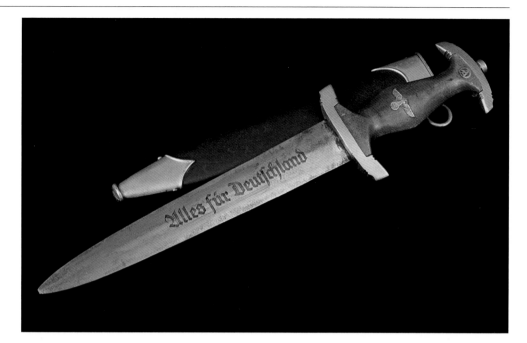

Third Reich SA (Sturmabteilung, Storm Detachment, 'Brown Shirts') dagger presented to 'accepted' members of the SA. Even rarer than this desirable model are the versions bearing the signature of the SA leader Ernst Roehm on the blade reverse. These signed versions were presentation pieces that would have been issued to a chosen few before his assassination in 1934.

our knowledge of events on the Somme or at Isandlwana, for example. However, amateur digging often disturbs buried bodies or reveals items which offer no accurate means of dating or specification.

EDGED WEAPONS

But another established field, however, the collecting of edged weapons remains unchanged and attracts its own enthusiasts. Because of their durability, these survive longer than cloth or leather artefacts, enabling collectors to own objects of far greater age than those owned by military uniform aficionados. Probably the most popular edged weapon for collectors is the bayonet.

Many of the collectors and re-enactors who own 'deacts' – nonfiring rifles – also own bayonets linked to the weapons. Probably the most popular is the standard issue 17in bayonet designed to fit that staple of the British army, the .303 Lee-Enfield, of which a staggering 17 million were produced. The famous knife bayonet of Great War vintage gave soldiers setting out on a bayonet charge with the redoubtable SMLE Mk III rifle, developed as long ago as 1903, a remarkable 6ft reach. No wonder few opponents waited around when charged by a section of screaming Tommies. Collectors of such bayonets are also likely to possess the spike bayonet or 'pig sticker', introduced in 1941 when the Mk III was deemed obsolete and replaced by the improved

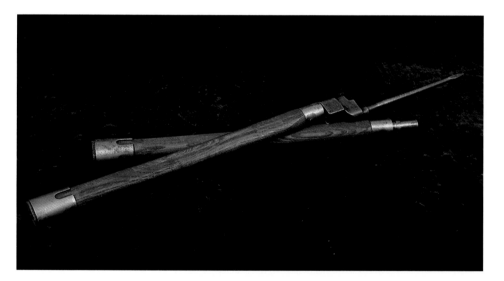

ABOVE: Two second-pattern entrenching tool handles for the British army two-piece entrenching tool. Originally introduced as part of the M1908 pattern web equipment, in 1941 it was reintroduced for fitting to the newer M1937 pattern equipment. The handle has a mounting designed to fit the new spike bayonet (the 'pig sticker') for the No.IV rifle and combined was intended as a rudimentary mine probe. This suddenly became a requirement following the demise of the 17in-long bayonet of Great War fame, made obsolete when the previous SMLE No.III rifle was superseded.

RIGHT: Skewer blade from a socket bayonet modified to fit onto a wooden pole. One of the improvised pikes used by the Local Defence Volunteers in lieu of rifles during the early summer of 1940. One of the most evocative British Second World War home front souvenirs.

Mk IV. They are also likely to own the No.9 Mk 1 bayonet, the more traditional, 'knife-edged' weapon that replaced the short-lived spike after the Second World War.

The *SA* dagger illustrated in this book is highly desirable although, ironically, not very valuable. Ernst Roehm's organization numbered nearly a million men at its height – each was issued with a dagger. However, the early ones, before its creator was removed during the 'Night of the Long Knives', bore Roehm's signature. Although thousands were dumped lest invading Soviet soldiers got the wrong idea by association, those

bearing his name realize the highest prices. As always, scarcity influences price. The one previously ubiquitous weapon but which did not survive the Great War in quantity was the Lewis gun. Those that were traded in the collectors' market achieved record prices. However, recently a hundred pristine examples of this famous machine gun came to light when the Kingdom of Nepal decided to dispose of its arsenal. Interestingly, this arms depot had, since the end of the nineteenth century when it was under British mandate, been the depository for numerous obsolete firearms.

Member of the L.D.V. in civilian clothes with brassard. He is wearing a British MkII steel helmet and is shouldering a wooden training rifle. He stands in front of a 'Beaverette' armoured car - an expedient national defence measure used mainly by the Home Guard.

8 Ephemera

BEFORE THE SECOND WORLD WAR

One definition of ephemera is: 'Items designed to last only for a short time, such as programmes or posters'. For collectors of militaria, 'ephemera' cover a slightly wider range of items including magazines, newspapers and even books. However, in wartime, the numerous official instructions and notices distributed among the civilian population, together with countless service handbooks, supplements and training manuals were also ephemeral in nature.

Mass-produced ephemeral material was not much in evidence before the Industrial Revolution and most notably the introduction of cheap high-speed lithographic printing. While there are still some First World War gems available such as aircraft spotters' guides, illustrating the silhouettes of not only enemy biplanes but also *Zeppelin* airships, or instructions telling Kitchener's soldiers how to behave when in contact with French civilians, for example, these pieces are few and far between. Indeed, examples of Great War ephemera, whether produced by the allies or the Central Powers, are now not far off being a century old. Being generally cheaply produced, the paper used was often of low quality; paper manufacturing technology in the early twentieth century was then still in its infancy and the bleaches used to clean the pulp often contributed to early deterioration, even the best of surviving Great War printed material is now likely to be yellow and brittle.

Although there are collections of First World War ephemera, as there from the inter-war years (the fabled 'goolie chits' carried by RAF pilots flying along the North-West Frontier, designed to encourage tribesmen to return downed aviators intact in return for a reward, being highly collectable) and post-Second World War items (Korean, Vietnam and Gulf War propaganda pieces being top of the list), it has to be said that most collectors seek items from the Second World War.

OFFICIAL PUBLICATIONS

Many official orders and training supplements were produced in a state of emergency, government instructions to 'Stay Put!' or how to achieve 'Beating the Invader' were hurriedly produced because of the prospect of an invasion in 1940. Manuals for the P.17 Springfield rifle, purchased from storage in the USA for distribution to the Home Guard, were short-lived, like the .300 calibre rifle (the British service rifle calibre was .303). These items, as with instructions for Local Defence Volunteers (LDV), temporary predecessors of the Home Guard, or information regarding the ill-fated sound-locators, predecessors and possible cover ruse for radar, were produced in relatively small numbers and for only a short time. They are consequently quite rare.

One of the criticisms frequently levelled at collectors and hobbyists in general is that they tend to be somewhat myopic, unable to grasp the complete picture. It is true that enthusiasts can be short-sighted, perhaps unable to see their passion in its true context and tending to get things out of proportion. If so, one way of making sense of a Second World War badge or uniform collection is to study the plethora of printed material produced alongside such items. Only by understanding Field Service Regulations will an enthusiast truly appreciate the sense behind military procedure. A Royal Engineer's Field Service manual explains the relevance of the trades and skills depicted in cloth and metal insignia which combine to create a modern, mechanized army, and an examination of W.D. & H.O. Wills's ARP

A typical British Second World War 'kitchen front' arrangement. Despite a reliance on rationing, dried milk and recycling, the diet of the average Briton was a healthy if frugal one since and rationing at least helped to encourage a levelling of the classes. Although a healthy Black Market thrived, and those with money and influence no doubt managed to secure more, curiously, it was those who were living in rural areas, often the poorest financially, who by virtue of being closest to the land, actually did better than most.

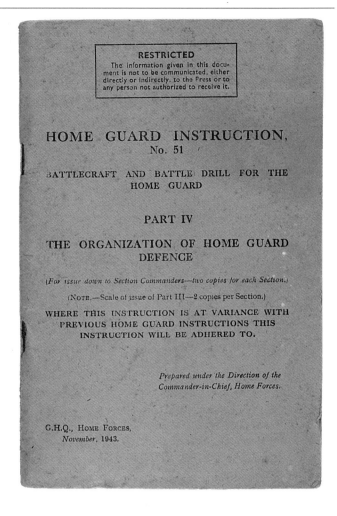

'Stay Where You Are', a Ministry of Information leaflet published on behalf of the War Office and Ministry of Home Security, urging Britons to stay at home in the event of a German invasion in 1940. With fresh memories of the debacle in France and the Low Countries during May and early June, the government did not want refugees clogging the roads should German troops actually make landfall in England.

A fascinating Home Guard Instruction booklet (No.51), dating from 1943. Its pages are filled with details about roadblocks, street fighting, ambushes, house clearance and static defence. The spreads shown here describe the manufacture of an SIP grenade (a type of Molotov cocktail), how to handle the Home Guards' unique Smith gun, use of the army's toggle rope and a description of the best way to defend a house. Almost anything to do with the Home Guard is now highly collectable.

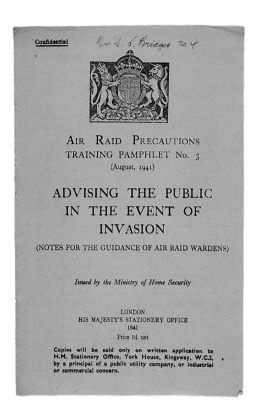

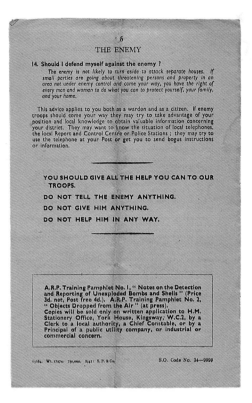

This fascinating document dates from 1941 and is evidence that Britain was not off the hook as far as an invasion was concerned, Hitler having only 'postponed' Operation Seelöwe while he concentrated on his new enemy Soviet Russia. This document was produced to give instruction to air raid wardens on dealing with a frightened and a naturally curious public, should the Wehrmacht yet invade in the summer of 1941.

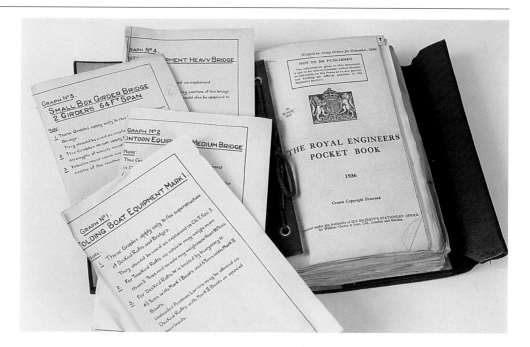

A complete Royal Engineers' pocket book from 1936. It is still quite easy to find the individual component sections, but leatherette-bound examples, which include the original pull-outs in a pocket inside the back cover, like this one, are increasingly rare.

cigarette card series, published in the late 1930s, encourages a better understanding of the civil defence and auxiliary organizations that later supplemented the regular forces during the Blitz.

The collecting of wartime ephemera has advantages beyond the educational, of course. To store dozens of old leaflets and magazines is considerably easier than to conserve combat gear such as battle-dress blouses and greatcoats. Although the most collectable items of printed ephemera are those produced in only limited numbers, many publications – most noticeably the

famous Stationery Office (HMSO) series – were printed in quantity. Their very number means that great many have survived and consequently they are still affordable and may be found at boot sales and in charity shops for a few pounds. It is worth snapping up originals, although since the fiftieth anniversary of the Second World War's end facsimiles have been produced by HMSO, a testament to their quality and desirability and an indication of demand, so why not own an original while you can?

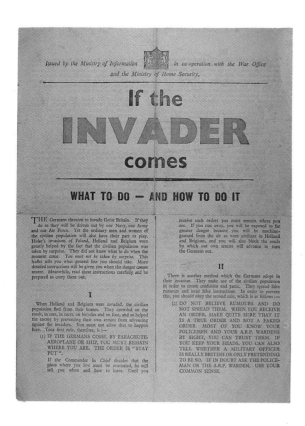

'The Germans threaten to invade Britain. If they do so they will be driven out by our Navy, our Army and our Air Force', so began one of the most rare and evocative civilian communications produced by the Ministry of Information: If the Invader Comes. What to do – and How to Do It.

The sudden appearance of pilotless bombs (V1s) immediately following the D-Day landings and then the even more terrifying the supersonic V2 rockets, were great shocks to the British. This NFS Benevolent Fund pamphlet published in 1945 went some way to demystifying these technologically advanced 'vengeance weapons'.

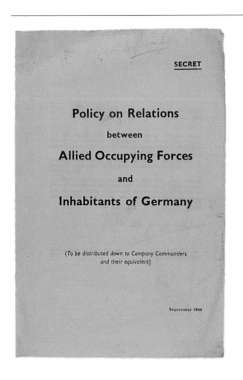
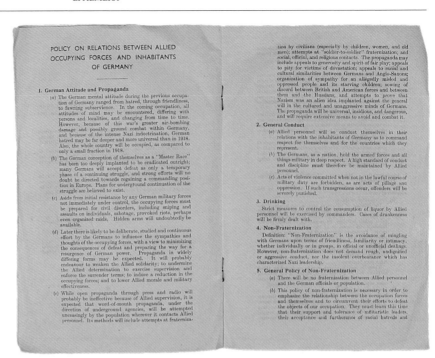

Produced in September 1944, this document, telling allied troops how to deal with the inhabitants of occupied Germany, was somewhat premature. The failure at Arnhem and the subsequent German Christmas offensive in the Ardennes (the Battle of the Bulge) meant that allied soldiers would not enter the heart of the Reich until the following year.

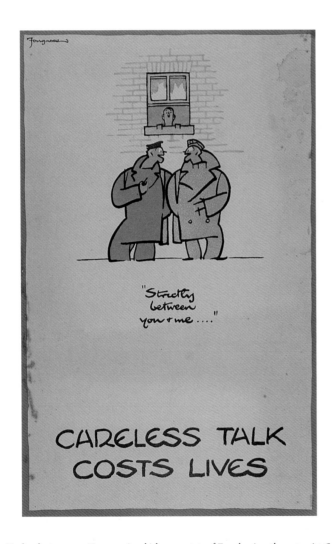

Under the pen name 'Fougasse', which was a type of French mine, the cartoonist Cyril Bird designed these famous posters in 1939. There are others in the series, notably Hitler and Goering eavesdropping into a passenger's conversation on the London Underground, but these two originals, in good condition, now command premium prices at auction.

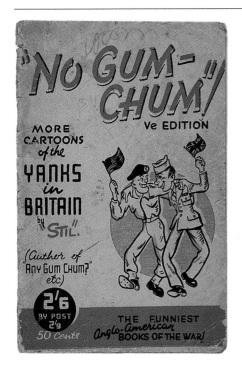

ABOVE: 'Got any gum chum?', British children would cry out to passing American GIs. This book of cartoons, published as part of the VE celebrations, is an affectionate look at the 'Friendly Invasion' of Britain by American servicemen.

RIGHT: This Second World War US interservices poster warned of the perils of taking holiday photographs which might reveal the whereabouts of allied ships.

WHO DO YOU THINK YOU'RE KIDDING, MR HITLER?

As is the general rule, Second World War militaria objects related to the Third Reich are of the highest value. This does not necessarily mean German-produced material, of course, although materials that survived the destruction of Hitlerite Germany are rarer than the proverbial hen's teeth. The shock caused by Britain's declaration of war on 3 September 1939 was visceral, after the long period of appeasement the British felt duped by 'Herr Hitler'. Consequently, and much to the embarrassment of the far right, British publishers produced a flurry of satirical pamphlets, novelties and song sheets, depicting the *Führer* in a satirical light. The words and music to Annette Mills's famous 'Adolf' can still be found today. Featuring a photograph of the popular radio comedian Arthur Askey, who recorded the song, the cover of this foolscap-sized song-sheet shows Hitler sprawled across Old Bill's bended knee as Bruce Bairnsfather's famous Great War soldier 'Old Bill', wallops him with a hob-nailed ammunition boot, and another satirical publication of the period that can still be found in second-hand bookshops is the *Daily Sketch*'s war-relief fundraiser *Struwwelhitler*,

costing just 1s.6d. (about 7p). This booklet was a parody of the famous German children's story *Struwwelpeter*. *Adolf in Blunderland*, a less than subtle parody of Lewis Carroll's classic about Alice, was illustrated by Norman Mansbridge; it rather viciously portrayed the then Prime Minister Neville Chamberlain as the novel's blue, hookah-smoking caterpillar perched on a toadstool emblazoned with Hitler's conquests (Hitler was depicted as Alice).

On a more serious note other pieces of early Second World War ephemera featuring Hitler are even more collectable. Broadsheets, printed with the text of his famous 'Last Appeal to Reason' speech, which drifted from the clouds over England in July 1940, are perhaps the rarest of all. Printed with the text of a speech he delivered to the *Reichstag* on 19 July in which he implored the British to rebel against their 'bourgeois' government. Many copies of this quite fragile publication fell straight out of the bomb bays of Heinkels and Dorniers and straight into the hands of Britons who promptly used them as lavatory paper – to preserve them was considered unpatriotic, but surviving examples deserve to be saved.

Die Wehrmacht, *like the* Luftwaffe's Adler *and the popular* Signal *this German wartime magazine extolled the actions of Nazi fighting men. Just how much Hitler's Reich had expanded can be seen top right where the price of the magazine in each occupied land is printed.*

Published throughout Second World War until 1945, Der Adler *was the Luftwaffe's propaganda magazine. Until the USA joined the war in late 1941, the magazine was published in German and English. With a Heinkel He 111 bomber on its cover, this is a French edition from 1942, featuring an article showing an RAF Blenheim bomber being shot down over the North Sea.*

ABOVE: As in Britain, so in Germany there was a thriving market for aircraft recognition books.

RIGHT: This magazine, the Kölnische Illustrierte ('Cologne Illustrated'), dates from May 1940; on its cover two German infantrymen are shown pausing for a cigarette. Inside is evidence of the anti-Semitism prevailing in German culture.

ABOVE: Catalogue to a Berlin art fair staged at the same time as the 1936 Olympics. Considered dull and unimaginative, 'acceptable' German art from this period was largely representational and mimicked the art of ancient Rome and Greece.

RIGHT: A rare Second World War handbook describing the uniforms, equipment, drill and combat procedures of the German army.

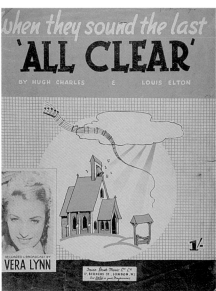

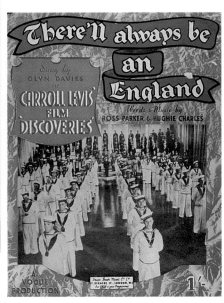

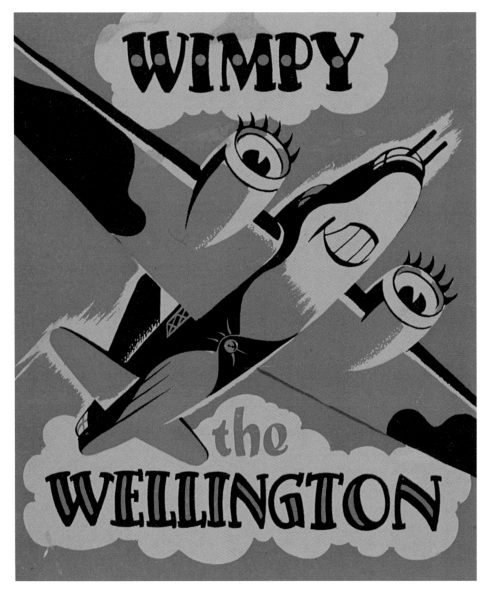

ABOVE: *The collecting of sheet music is still relatively easy. Thousands of pieces were produced. Left to right, the piano solo played as part of the sound track to the wartime film* The Way to the Stars, *starring Michael Redgrave and John Mills; 'When they sound the last all clear', sheet music and lyrics to the wartime song made famous by Vera Lynn; sheet music to the stirring song by Parker and Charles, 'There'll always be an England'.*

LEFT: *Children's books such as this one,* Wimpy the Wellington, *by F. Herbert, with evocative illustrations by the cartoonist Philip Zec, admirably conjure up the spirit of wartime.*

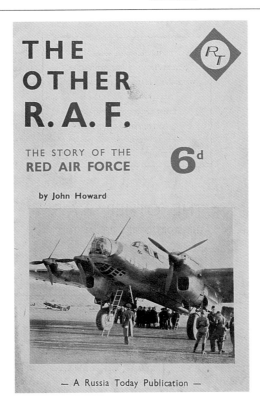

RIGHT: The other RAF – the Red Air Force. *Typical of the numerous British publications celebrating the activities and achievements of the Soviet ally.*

FAR RIGHT: With the Home Guard, *by Capt Fine. Wartime books are still quite common, but finding them with their dust jackets is not so easy.*

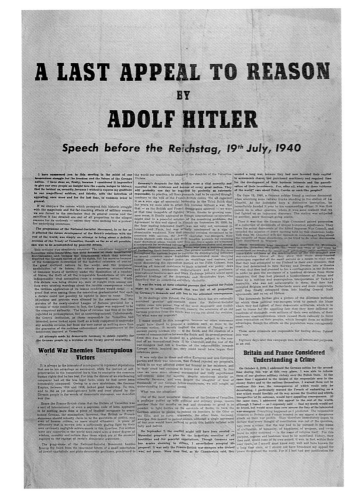

Very rare surviving example of the text of Hitler's 'Last Appeal to Reason' speech as delivered to the Reichstag on 19 July 1940. Any hopes that he might have had about this olive branch were soon dispelled. Dropped in their thousands by the Luftwaffe, the British press made fun of the communication and many householders used the leaflets as lavatory paper.

THE HOME FRONT

It may be difficult to appreciate today, but by the late 1930s civilians feared an airborne gas attack in precisely the same way that later generations feared the four-minute warning and a nuclear strike. Following the deadly use of chlorine, phosgene and lewisite (mustard gas) on the Western Front during the Great War, most people assumed that gas would be used again, but this time delivered against the civil population from the air by the new breed of high-speed, monoplane bombers; Stanley Baldwin, Prime Minister before Chamberlain, held that 'the bomber will always get through'. Consequently, an enormous amount of printed material supported the more tangible aspects of air raid precautions, such as the ubiquitous gas masks and blast-protected, taped windows. Leaflets advised people to carry their gas masks at all times, how to build a bomb-proof shelter (preferably under the stairs, which was considered the most robust place inside a house) and how to tape and seal gaps around doors and windows to prevent the entry of poisonous gas. Most communications, especially the series of Civil Defence Public Information leaflets, were serious but some, like the seaside postcards advising nudists to at least don a gas mask, were frivolous. Many of these publications may still be found and provide the ideal supplement to a collection of larger objects such as respirators, first aid kits and decontamination outfits. Combined, these items tell the story of a harrowing period in Britain's history.

Although many women joined the ranks of the ATS, the Women's Land Army, the WAAF and ARP units, among numerous other national organizations, in the Second World War, with most able-bodied men drafted into the forces, the majority of women stayed at home. The exigencies of total war imposed severe restrictions on the supply of imported goods and hence many home-produced goods were directed to the war effort, the rationing of food, fuel and clothing was the result.

But, with great ingenuity, cookery writers and chefs devised numerous recipes to help housewives to eke out the meagre

National anxieties in Britain about the enemy use of poison gas during air raids inspired this late 1930s set of lead figures representing an ARP anti-gas decontamination crew (Taylor & Barrett).

rations and make the most of a limited supply of common ingredients and booklets appeared advising on the most economical use of ration coupons (there were even quiz booklets explaining the rules behind the amounts established for clothing, footwear, cloth and, important for 1940s housewives, knitting yarn). By combining a selection of the numerous publications from the so-called 'kitchen-front' with wartime editions of women's magazines and ration books an interesting and increasingly valuable collection may be built up.

Another popular area in which to collect relates to fashion. Women of all ages like to look attractive, an attitude that wartime restrictions did little to dent and, even if they could not

buy the latest fashions as before, they could at least 'Make Do and Mend', as the slogan of the time put it. They could also create clothing from scratch by using fabrics and textiles perhaps put away before hostilities began. Not surprisingly, many patterns costing 6d. (about 2.5p) can still be found. These range from 'War-time Renovations', showing how old garments could be transformed into the latest cuts, to 'Economy Frocks', encouraging women to make modest dresses from the cheapest available fabrics. Collectors not inclined to opt for such items might at least consider 'New Woollies for our Sailors, Soldiers and Airman', which featured pictures of fighting men on its cover – albeit wearing rather camp cardigans and Fair Isle sweaters.

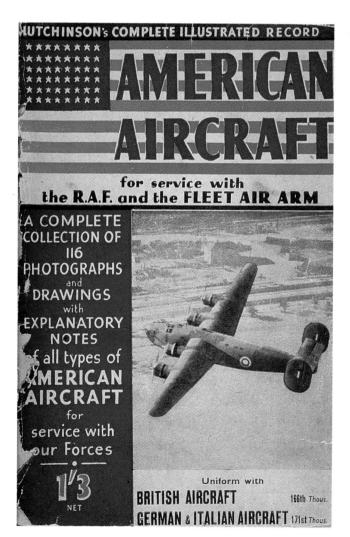

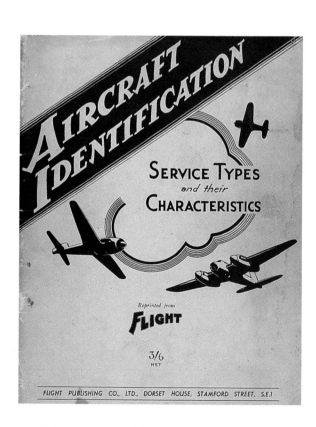

ABOVE: This British spotter's guide featured silhouettes taken from the pages of the famous British aircraft periodical Flight.

LEFT: With so many US aircraft in Britain from 1942 onwards, air-minded British youth demanded recognition books describing American warplanes. This publication by Hutchinson's was in a series that included British and Axis aircraft types. Such was the popularity of both of these titles that combined they had sold over 300,000 copies by the time the volume on American aircraft was produced.

BRITISH,
FRENCH AND GERMAN
<u>AIRCRAFT.</u>

Because of their short range the identification of enemy aircraft (other than Zeppelins) was not as critical to British civilians during the Great War. However, this did not stop publishers from cashing in on this fledgling craze. This booklet from 1916 detailed allied and enemy types. By 1918 however, enemy aircraft such as Gotha bombers could be increasingly seen over southern Britain.

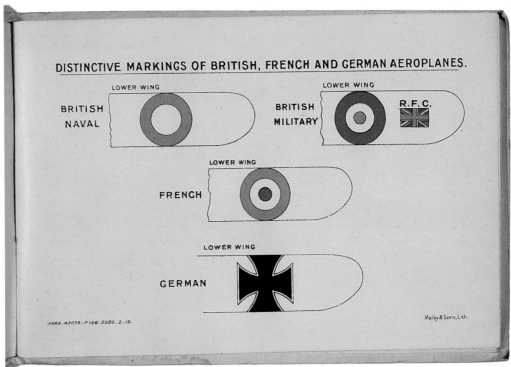

ABOVE: *A selection of aircraft spotting guides, an identification model of a Bristol Blenheim and an observer's chest microphone and headset.*

RIGHT: *Raphael Tuck's* ABC of Aeroplane Spotting, *featuring an illustration of the Prime Minister Winston Churchill as a pugilistic Bristol Beaufighter; this Second World War publication encouraged youngsters to recognize British aircraft by colouring in illustrations.*

A selection of early Second World War boys' toys, including a rare Dinky trade box, as supplied to toyshops, containing of six silver Bristol Blenheims; a Dinky Fairey Battle (front left) and a Spitfire are also featured.

A superb tin-plate toy Heinkel He 111 bomber manufactured by the famous Lehmann family firm, established in Brandenburg in 1881. Although infamous as the principal Luftwaffe bomber during the Blitz, the machine had been a workhorse of Goering's air-fleets for years before. The example shown is finished in the splinter camouflage more typical of the Condor Legion's involvement in the Spanish Civil War.

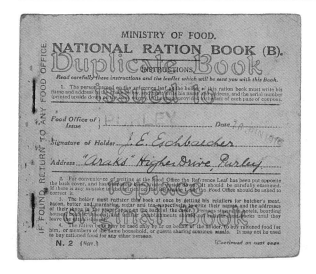

ABOVE: *Second World War British ration books are still relatively easy to find, however, collectors should beware, most examples actually date from the late 1940s or the early 1950s – rationing continued long after VJ Day. However, surviving examples of ration books from the Great War are extremely rare; this one dates from 1919, evidence that British agricultural imports had not immediately returned to normal after November 1918.*

RIGHT: *Early wartime British petrol coupons ('Not valid after September 30th 1940').*

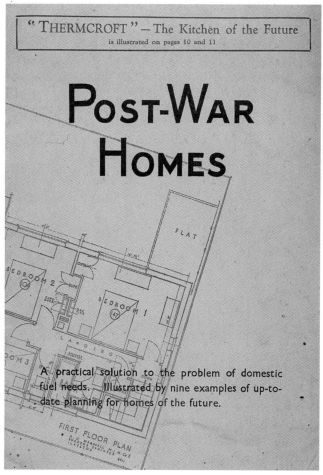

Preserves from the Garden, *published in 1940 by HMSO on behalf of the Ministry of Agriculture and Fisheries. Once commonplace, good examples of evocative period ephemera such as this are becoming scarce.*

Post-War Homes, *a commercially produced pamphlet describing the kind of well-heated, insulated homes, to be built to replace the numerous slums destroyed or damaged by the ravages of 'total war'.*

SOUVENIRS AND TRENCH ART

Not strictly ephemeral, because they were certainly intended to last a long time, this chapter is probably the best place in which to discuss wartime souvenirs and 'trench art'. It is a truism of the military life that a great deal of time is spent waiting for something to happen. Many old soldiers remember wartime service as being long periods of tedium interspersed with sudden moments of terrifying activity. While waiting for the order to go 'over the top' or advance towards a distant objective on a map, soldiers of every generation whiled away the time reading, singing bawdy barrack-room ballads or writing home to loved ones, among other distractions. Some of the most poignant relics of both world wars are the delightful embroidered postcards soldiers posted home. These delicate, often filigree objects, contrast dramatically with the tired, battledress-clad men who wrote them. It is equally moving to discover that lace-decorated cards, with the message 'Souvenir of the BEF', were posted by British soldiers stationed in France in both 1914 and 1940.

Collecting such sentimental relics also helps the military enthusiast to gain a fuller picture of the soldier's life. Although often heavily censored or containing few details about the location or activities of the writer, what words there are often paint a more realistic picture of military service than countless biographies by distant commanders could ever archive. Examples of such communications, posted just before a seismic event such as the battle of the Somme in 1916 or the Dunkirk evacuation in 1940, also contribute to our contextual understanding of military history.

Although 'trench art' was created in the Second World War (there is a fine example of such a piece produced by an *Afrika Korps* soldier in this book), the heyday of such handiwork occurred on the Western Front during the 1914–18 war. With such a vast amount of ordnance being lobbed to and fro across no-man's land by the opposing armies, it is hardly surprising that bored soldiers decided to fashion some of the thousands of spent shell cases into battlefield souvenirs. Consequently, unwanted brass cases were fashioned into a wide range of containers, vases and, commonly, ashtrays. These objects were decorated with often quite sophisticated, etched designs revealing naïve messages such as a 'Souvenir of the Great War' or 'Allies in arms'. Prisoners of war obviously had plenty of time on their hands. Like their colleagues on the front line, they fashioned souvenirs from whatever materials they could lay their hands on. While not of the sophistication perhaps of the ship models, painstakingly fashioned from bone and ivory by Napoleonic prisoners, examples of the handiwork of twentieth-century POWs are still enlightening. Italian prisoners, for example, having mostly demonstrated their willingness to comply with the rules of their captors and, as a result being trusted to work on the land in Britain, fraternizing peacefully with British civilians, had better access to materials needed to make toys and dolls. These craft works were often exchanged for rations. Interestingly, however, one of us (A.W.) recalls his mother telling him that, when she was a child growing up in central London, by far the best place to obtain sweets and fancies was from the Italian prisoners.

Princess Mary's Christmas smoker's gift tin from 1914. Along with a Christmas card, it included cigarettes and tobacco.

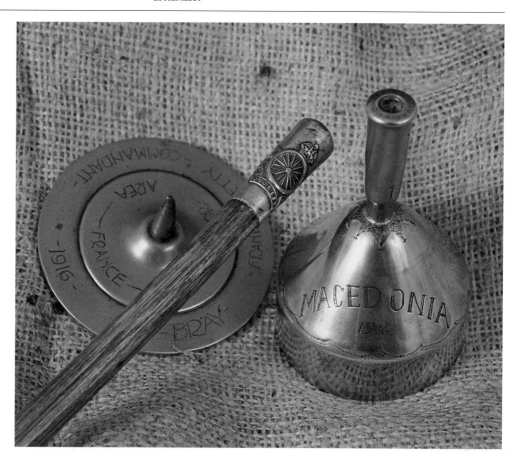

RIGHT: *Two examples of 'trench art': a bell and paper spike fabricated from inert munitions inscribed with place names and dates of engagements and a swagger stick whose top bears the insignia of the Army Cyclist Corps.*

ABOVE: *French soldier's portable drinking cup dated 1939. Individualized by its owner through the addition of engraving showing where he was serving and probably intended as a souvenir for friends or relatives. This kind of handy work was commonplace in the French army at this time and many relics from this period show a deft creativity that perhaps belies the duties of the owner.*

RIGHT: *An unusual piece of 'trench art' from the Second World War – a shell case engraved by a member of the* Afrika Korps.

This home-made toy tank was fashioned in the early 1920s, its style being a combination of Great War designs and the armoured vehicles with turrets that followed shortly after.

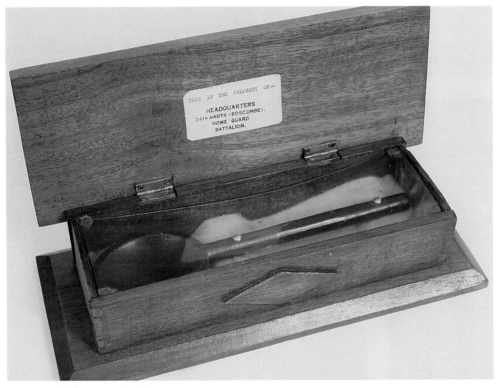

LEFT: Wooden spoon awarded to an unlucky recipient serving with the 24th Hants (Boscombe) Battalion of the Home Guard.

BELOW: Selection of tiny figures depicting servicemen from each of the Third Reich's armed forces mounted on pins to wear as badges. These were sold to raise funds for troops on the Eastern Front as part of the annual Winterhilfe campaigns.

'Firex' brand fire extinguisher. A grenade, designed to be thrown at the base of a fire, it was one of the many halon-containing devices that proliferated as fear of the potential havoc to be wrought by enemy bombers gripped the nation. The start of the Blitz in the autumn of 1940 proved that people and buildings could withstand the 'aerial terror'.

CHILDREN'S BOOKS

An area that is often overlooked by militaria collectors is that of wartime children's books. Many good examples of these survive – all ephemeral in nature because, like Richmal Crompton's *William the Dictator* (Newnes, 1938) and *William and A.R.P.* (Newnes, 1939), they were really relevant only during their own time. There were many short-lived developments during the war whose impact, though brief, was sufficient for them to be immortalized in children's books and periodicals.

One in particular was the barrage balloon, which was soon made redundant by the various technological advances in aerial warfare. In an effort to demystify these potentially scary and sinister objects they were humanized; books such as *Bulgy the Barrage Balloon, Boo-Boo the Barrage Balloon,* and the more originally titled *Blossom the Brave Balloon,* were all illustrated with cheerful cartoons and accompanied by a narrative that encouraged young readers to bond with the tethered inflatables floating above the country's factories and dock installations.

RIGHT: The cover of Bulgy the Barrage Balloon, *an illustrated children's story by Enid Marx, which attempted to humanize the giant inflatables that youngsters saw floating overhead.*

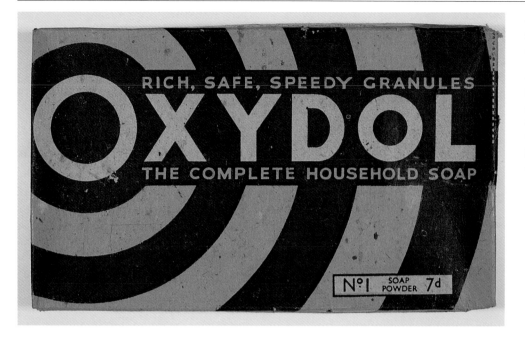

In Britain during wartime overt displays of patriotism could be the decider between one brand and another. Oxydol washing powder stole a lead over its competitors by associating itself with the war effort. Packaged in War Standard economy cardboard, the brand claimed to be as good as ever, but, because its packaging saved on precious resources, it provided 'Two More Nails in Hitler's Coffin!'

BELOW: Cover of popular wartime monthly, Lilliput. It shows how in total war, beachcombers could make some quite unusual finds.

PUBLICATIONS HELPING TO INTEGRATE

With so many troops from overseas in Britain during the Second World War it is not surprising that much material was published designed to help them to integrate into a very different society from their own. Alongside booklets advising troops from the USA and the Dominions about customs in what one humorist called 'Occupied England', there were numerous unofficial publications such as *Got Any Gum Chum?* and *Where's the Garbage Can?* which attempted to bridge the gap between often quite disparate cultures.

PATRIOTIC PACKAGING

It is beyond the scope of this book to consider all the ephemera worth collecting. However, enthusiasts might also choose to track down examples of surviving packaging. Soap powder boxes, such as Oxydol for example, carried patriotic messages:

Two More Nails In Hitler's Coffin! – To save cardboard for the Nation we have reduced the size of this packet. The cardboard saved from this packet is enough to make two cartridge wads. The weight of Oxydol inside is the same by fixed national standards. You are buying the same grand Oxydol value, the same rich granulated soap.

In total war, everyone did his or her bit.

9 Checking for Authenticity and Detecting Fakes

It is no good spending your hard-earned cash on an item of alleged authenticity only to discover that it isn't original at all.

FAKERY

However, 'fakes' in themselves need a degree of definition, they may be either simple, mass-produced copies of cloth and metal insignia, which will catch out only the inexperienced by incorrect description (and, anyway, perhaps started life as clearly labelled reproductions for use by re-enactors), or, as regards metal insignia, sophisticated 'restrikes', dishonestly intended to deceive. So things are not as straightforward as one might expect.

The question of originality is also relevant. Sometimes items are combined to make a part of a uniform more interesting. This is usually achieved by the addition of insignia to a headdress or uniform, all genuine but never actually together at the period suggested. Equally, steel helmets are prone to the addition of decals and painted insignia to make them more interesting and valuable.

Although proportionally small in number as regards military collectables, as with all antiques, the most troublesome fakes are the ones that are completely scratch-made. These copies of rare items, usually uniforms, are designed to catch out enthusiasts. In certain areas, such as Nazi German cloth and metal insignia, this can be especially problematical; once they have been artificially aged it can be difficult to tell them from the real things. Equally, once a good fake has passed through more than one pair of hands people can become more convinced of its authenticity. Collectors should also be mindful of items that seem to be *too reasonably* priced, or available in infeasibly large quantities when they should be rare.

BE ON YOUR GUARD

No matter how much you want something, particularly if it is apparently inexpensive, stop and think. Do not let your

'It happened here!' As was famously stage-managed in the occupied Channel Islands, this image shows a contrived propaganda image with German troops consulting a hapless British Bobby in Parliament Square. A German army officer (Oberleutnant) and an infantry NCO (Unterfeldwebel) speak to the police officer who wears a closed collar tunic and dark peaked cap with white metal constabulary insignia. Of note is the white infantry, inverted 'V' piping on the NCO's Feldmutz and the other ranks' buckle and belt compared to the officer's pattern two-tongue buckle and brown belt, both typical of the early war period. Both the officer and the NCO have been awarded the infantry assault badge for service in combat. The Oberleutnant is a recipient of both the Iron Cross 2nd class (ribbon to button) and 1st class (on breast pocket).

Selection of RN insignia adjacent to some relevant Second World War HMSO publications (still relatively easy to locate), a period novel by Nicholas Monsarrat and The Navy, *Aug. 1943. Identification of naval cloth badges from the top down: petty officer (crown and crossed anchor); leading seaman (anchor); good conduct stripes; cap badge (rating class ii); gunnery (crossed guns); leading torpedo man; torpedo man; signaller (winged lightning); visual signaller (flags); sail maker; physical training instructor; stoker (3 props); airframe mechanic (4 props); motor mechanic (2 props); supply branch ('S' senior rate with crown); diver and bugler.*

enthusiasm and eagerness to own (a real problem with collectors we know) run away with you. Be sure that you have no doubts and, if possible, get a second opinion. We have no wish to do military dealers a disservice, but it is far more likely that you will be presented with an amended or faked item at a specialist enthusiasts' fair than a more reasonably priced item sold in isolation at a car boot sale. There is big money in military collectables and genuine items are becoming scarce, so, buyers beware.

Experience does count. Sometimes this is an inexplicable, subconscious 'awareness' of what's right. Is it as old as it purports to be? It is actually quite difficult to age an item reliably and almost impossible to achieve the 'smell' of age; study the apparent effects of age and wear – do the scratches conform to the position of the attachment or slung equipment that would have caused the wear in the first place? If something is allegedly battle-worn and a survivor of the muddy soil of Vimy Ridge, would the delicate fabric backing really have survived so well? How has a piece of khaki serge, stored unnoticed for ninety years, really survived the predatory attentions of moths? Though fewer and farther between than they were, many reputable

militaria dealers offer guarantees of some kind, especially with higher priced items of equipment such as nineteenth-century helmets or Third Reich regalia. Similarly, most reputable auction houses will refund the price paid for an item if it can be shown that, in reality, it does not have the authenticity promised by the company's catalogue listing.

As time goes on, the current batch of re-enactors' uniforms of a higher standard, perhaps in approximately twenty years' time, will bear authentic wear and begin to appear as 'of a certain age'. Certainly, there was a period when fake cloth insignia could be scanned with UV light to show man-made polyester fibre, but with the proliferation of materials coming from the Far East – where natural fibres are still much in daily use – detection is now more difficult. However, on the balance of probability, obscure pieces of uniform and insignia, appearing in isolation, are less likely to be faked. Provenance is everything, a battledress blouse or a 'battle bowler' unearthed from Granddad's attic and which can be attributed to a serving ancestor is doubtless genuine, but the *SS* camo smock bought from a West End dealer perhaps less so.

10 Preservation and Display

All collectors of militaria know that the stress induced by the search and final payment for that long-coveted item of kit continues long after ownership. Decay is a constant and unchanging fact: those who possess old bayonets, daggers and field equipment are well acquainted with the damage that corrosion can do to such items. And then there are uniforms that can be eaten by living things such as moths and the 'woolly bear'. The preservation of treasured gains is a never-ending and often time-consuming business.

TEXTILES

The first and most important conservation method to adopt if you want your collection to remain in tip-top condition is to keep everything at a constant temperature and humidity. This relates to items stored behind glass for display as well as those kept in trunks and cupboards that may be occasionally retrieved for use for re-enactment. The biggest danger arises when uniforms and equipment are brought in from the cold to a warm, centrally heated environment and vice versa. The sudden rise or drop in temperature generates water moisture, condensation. This hastens the development of rust and the sudden dampness will oxidize and corrode metal in contact with a uniform, leaving marks that are almost impossible to shift. Extreme damp will lead to the appearance of mould and ultimately rot the uniform fabric.

With woollen uniforms it is always advisable to have them cleaned before incorporating them into a collection. Areas that are exceptionally dirty or sweaty act as a magnet to the even greater danger of the clothes-moth. Their eggs, difficult to detect with the naked eye, could be harboured by any piece of old clothing or woollen insignia you bring into your collection room or storage area. These and the woolly bear, a hazard specific to wool (the basis of many twentieth-century uniforms), can sneak up initially unnoticed, even in items on display, only later to be spotted once the damage has been done. Many collections lie dormant inside boxes and suitcases in dark places such as cupboards and attics. However, it takes only one contaminated host object to spread its infestation through objects put away and forgotten for months or years. Vigilance is the watchword.

But prevention is the better method: try to avoid inviting infestation in the first place. Thoroughly inspect items before storing them and, if in doubt, have them professionally cleaned. Make sure objects are properly stored in sealed boxes with no gaps to allow the access of tenacious insects. Mothballs or other repellent fragrances are really effective only for items stored in a wardrobe; decreasing in size and effectiveness as they turn into vapour, they need constant replacement.

If items of woollen clothing and insignia are on display they should be held in sealed cabinets, keeping them clean and free from dust. It is important to remember that the mites and insects which lay eggs while they munch away at you precious vintage uniforms are attracted to the dusty creases and folds of materials.

Wartime collectables can include valve radios, art deco lamps, newspapers and popular reading such as Howard Thomas's Brighter Blackout Book, as this tableau suggests.

LIGHT EFFECTS

If collections are on open display the effect of natural light falling on mannequins or display cases must be borne in mind. As every artist knows, colours are fugitive (owners of red cars also know how quickly the finish of their vehicles deteriorates after even a relatively short time). Direct sunlight leads to the most significant fading, not just for uniform items but also especially for printed ephemera such as posters and leaflets. What is the point in paying a premium price for a wartime National War Savings poster (and such items are now increasingly sought after) only to discover that of the printers' inks used only the least fugitive – cyan blue – remains? So be careful.

METALS

Collectors ought, one feels, to be entitled to think that steel helmets, perhaps the most robust of military collectables, would be impervious to decay or damage while in storage. Think again. While the shells are naturally remarkably resilient, the liners, often made of composite materials, including much rubber, can deteriorate. It is definitely not a good idea to stack old steel helmets one on top of another. If you do, after time the traces touching helmet liners will be imprinted, halo like, on top of the helmet shell. It is also inadvisable to stuff tissue paper inside

helmets on the assumption that this will protect the linings from any adjacent stored helmets. Old vulcanized rubber perishes with time and it can be frustrating seeing so much acid-free tissue paper moulded inside steel helmets. It is also particularly advisable to ensure that areas featuring delicate decals, printed or painted stencilling or camouflage paints are protected. They should not rub against the shells or chinstrap buckles of other helmets.

BADGES AND INSIGNIA

In fact, apart from the predatory activities of insects, the other main peril in the collecting and preserving of military collectables is wear and tear. Be careful how you store badges and insignia. Pins are relatively delicate and can be snapped off if badges are simply jumbled together in a box. Many collectors like to clean their badges, which, as they would when in use, tarnish quite rapidly. While not necessarily suggesting the application of a proprietary cleaner such as Brasso, beloved of generations of National Servicemen, less abrasive cleaners can be used to return the shine gently to a prized badge collection.

Buttons may be cleaned in the traditional army way, by the use of a cleaning stick that avoids the staining of any material they may be attached to, either as part of a uniform or a display

Second World War Royal Navy headdress and ephemeral items; includes: ratings' white- and black-topped hats; green oilskin hat (Canadian naval issue); black-topped, red-badged peak cap worn by ratings not dressed as seaman (in supply or victualling branches, for example); knitted woollen hat; Navy 'cap comforter' and finally a 1943 proofed anti-flash hood. In the centre are a selection of wartime embroidered and one printed cap tallies and a bosun's whistle and chain. All the above are arranged on a sailor's counterpane (barrack-room bedcover), bearing a crown and anchor device at its centre.

ARP signs: enamel wardens post sign, notice identifying storage place for a stirrup pump and white cloth banner indicating the presence of an unexploded bomb. Coming from the London area most typically associated with the Blitz makes these items highly desirable.

background. However, despite the temptation, the majority of collectors shun the use of lacquers, applied either by brush or aerosol spray. Although they inhibit oxidation, the cause of tarnishing in the first place, they often impart a rather artificial finish more redolent of the Stay-brite badges and buttons introduced in the 1960s.

STORAGE OF CLOTHING AND RUBBER ITEMS

Rubber items, such as gas masks and certain types of footwear or clothing, must be kept at a 'constant temperature' – that is, not too hot or too cold. They should also be stored away from damp atmospheric conditions to prevent deterioration. When packing such items away for storage, a covering of talcum powder will prevent the material from sticking to whatever it may come into contact with. Rubber items should not be compressed whilst in storage as this will cause distortion and, if the material is already weak, there will also be damage through cracking.

For long-term preservation, gas masks survive better when out of their original bags, boxes or tins. They can be put away opened out to prevent distortion from compression, and can be packed out with acid-free tissue paper to preserve their shape. However, it is worth putting this material inside a plastic pack if it is in direct contact with rubber; this will avoid it sticking to the vulcanized material, which is never 100 per cent stable. The same rule can also be applied to rubberized cotton items such as waterproofs and some headsets, which should not be subjected to temperature changes or compression.

Items of anti-gas clothing are perhaps the most problematical to store successfully, due to their sticky texture. Certainly the application of some silicone in the form of furniture polish reduces this stickiness; this is a tried and tested

'trick of the trade', but whether this will be appropriate in the long term is difficult to say!

Leather items that are already starting to deteriorate need to be stored in the same way as rubber items. There is a school of thought that if old leather generates a bloom of mould, there is still life in it. If affected by serious rot (that is, red rot), only heavy oiling with an appropriate dressing will help preserve the item as a relic.

STORAGE OF RUSTY METAL

Rusty metal fittings, particularly on webbing, can also present problems. They are awkward to clean in situ because oiling may contaminate the equipment fabric. When packing them, care must be taken to avoid contact with other parts of the webbing item in order to prevent rust marks from staining fabrics. The swift touch of 'rust-eating paint' will avert this, of course, but will then seriously compromise the originality of the piece. Similar difficulties can occur with steel buttons, fittings or insignia attached to uniforms, if they have begun to oxidize and deteriorate.

Be mindful, too, of cheap metal coat hangers. If clothes are hung in areas subject to temperature changes, this will in time create damaging rust marks.

MODERN AIDS TO STORAGE

Modern collectors have a great many materials to choose from to help them to protect precious items. Badges and medals can be safely stored in simple jiffy bags, available in a variety of sizes and larger items may be protected by copious amounts of bubble wrap.

Store things with forethought, keep them both clean and dry, and avoid sudden changes in temperature and humidity. Then your treasures will survive for years.

11 Buying and Selling

As we have mentioned before, apart from badges, it is becoming ever harder to find undiscovered stocks of authentic militaria, particularly material dating from the Great War and, increasingly, items from the Second World War. By their very nature rarities are a finite resource. But although not much new material turns up these days, there is still a brisk trade in militaria as the ownership of items and even complete collections changes hands. However, they now buy online, unlike until relatively recently when collectors requested typewritten lists, made a choice, posted a cheque and waited 'twenty-one days for delivery', a process which could take a couple of months.

DEALING: OLD STYLE

The internet has changed everything, its overwhelming extent uniting buyers and sellers worldwide. Unlike in the 'old days', when enormous trust was required by buyers in the accuracy of written descriptions, collectors surfing on-line benefit from the availability of photographs revealing the true quality of their intended purchases.

Of course, there are still traditional shops specializing in militaria, but not as many as there were. The rationalization that has taken place in the trade has now probably bottomed out. By a process of natural selection to ensure commercial viability, most of the survivors have combined costume hire with the sale

A barrack room kit inspection reconstruction where an RSM of the Royal Sussex Regiment and a captain of the Coldstream Guards inspect a soldier's bed layout. Of particular note is the unique Guards' pattern of officers' service dress without pleats on the upper pockets and without a bellows gusset on the lower pockets. In keeping with tradition, on the front of the tunic the regimental buttons are mounted in groups (twos for the Coldstream Guards). Note that he is a First World War veteran and has the Military Cross and on the bottom of his right sleeve four inverted chevrons denoting four years' service. Surviving Second World War officers' service dress is still relatively common. However, this is an interesting example of the type.

Selection of ARP, Civil Defence and Fire Service cloth insignia (Second World War and post-war): LARP ('L' denoting London) and ARP badges for soft headdress; Red Cross driver's qualification badge for sleeve; shoulder titles (Second World War and post-war), Second World War National Fire Service (NFS) and Civil Defence (CD) badges; post-war Auxiliary Fire Service (AFS) beret badge.

of traditional military collectables as part of their service. Likewise, the traditional auction house business, apart from fine, high-end items such as armour, nineteenth-century headdress and uniforms and Renaissance edged weapons, has been dealt a body blow by on-line auctions, most notably by eBay; most items of twentieth-century combat gear are now auctioned via the ether.

LEGAL IMPLICATIONS

Another concern for auctioneers, collectors and re-enactors alike is the provisions of the Violent Crime Reduction Act that received royal assent in November 2006. Intended to prevent criminals from using firearms of any sort, real or replica, the Act has implications for those buying or selling antique weapons, and especially those who possess deactivated weapons. The ownership of 'de-acts' is not solely the province of re-enactors, they are also an important feature of museum display. In a Museums Association article last year, Jonathan Ferguson, collections officer at the Imperial War Museum's Duxford site said:

> We are in discussions with the Home Office to allow us to import, purchase and make replica weapons. But even if we are granted an exemption, the Bill will mean the price of replica weapons will sky-rocket. An aircraft machine gun that currently costs £1,200 will be worth double on the advent of the Bill and, given that a World War II fighter plane takes eight such guns, our acquisitions budget simply won't stretch that far.

However, a spokesman for the Home Office has said that museums and re-enactment societies are being considered for exemption from the prohibitions of the Bill.

Hazel Blears, formerly a Minister of State at the Home Office whose then responsibilities included crime reduction and counter-terrorism, was asked during one of the Commons stages of the Bill by a Member about the concerns of a constituent of his who was a member of the Great War Society and unsure whether he would be able to take his deactivated Lee-Enfield rifle to France and Belgium to participate in the ninetieth anniversary of the Battle of the Somme in July 2006. However, it seems from Ms Blears's response that collectors of deactivated weapons could breathe a sigh of relief, 'If the weapons are deactivated, those people will be able to take part in their activity.' She went on to praise the good work done by re-enactors, espe-

cially with schoolchildren, 'taking part in living history lessons to try to bring history alive.'

At the higher end of the market, collectors of finer eighteenth- and nineteenth-century muzzle-loading and percussion-loading firearms are likely to be left alone also. This will be a relief for auction houses such as Bonham's who, some months before this manuscript was completed, sold a Scottish, all-metal, silver-decorated snaphaunce pistol manufactured in 1672 and part of the famous Keith Neal Collection for the princely sum of £78,000.

There will always be lucky finds in antique centres, charity shops and at car boot sales. But, the reality is that, and certainly in the case of the last, the dealers have usually already combed though the goods on sale at the most unearthly hour and plucked anything really worthwhile long before the average browser arrives. Bargains can still be found, but because of the many television programmes explaining the value of old items, most of us now probably have a pretty good idea of what something is worth. In Britain, charity shops are becoming much more aware, employing specialists who advise them about competitive pricing. The consequence is that now there are far smaller margins between the prices charged by charity shops for books and collectables and those levied by traditional antique and curio dealers.

DEALING: NEW STYLE

Nevertheless, the most exciting market is undoubtedly the on-line auction. To make the best of it, especially when selling, it pays to know a few facts. Although not the only internet auction site available, eBay is by far the most successful. Part of its success is its competitiveness when compared with traditional auctions. Sellers' commission rates are lower than those of the established auction houses, being on a reducing sliding scale. There is no hammer price commission levied on buyers, another economy. Being an innovator, eBay piloted many of the mechanisms now commonplace on-line. Regardless of your chosen e-commerce facilitator, however, there are several essentials necessary when buying or selling successfully, but many of these fundamentals have always applied to trading. The key to achieving commercial success with any enterprise is marketing, it makes no difference whether you have the most desirable object for sale – if no one knows that you are selling it. Consequently it is important to list your items accurately and, of course, in the

British Second World War Mk II ARP helmet for a member of a first aid party. The sign-written large lettering of this example is perhaps more typical of the ARP at the beginning of the war.

British Second World War Mk II civil defence chief warden white helmet with two black rank bars.

right place, which is the right category. But if you have something saleable and have described it accurately, the functionality of eBay in particular is so good that a prospective purchaser will quickly discover your treasure. To maximize your income, there is no real need to list an item classified as 'Rare, 1940 dated, chief warden's shrapnel helmet with expandable strap' in any category other than 'Second World War Home Front Militaria'. Keen enthusiasts will find it, believe us.

It is, however, worth pausing for a moment before you gamely snap a few digital pictures of your sale item. The explosion of affordable digital cameras in the 4-megapixel plus range, more than adequate for the display of images online (screen resolution being only 72dpi [dots per inch] remember), means

that it is simplicity itself to post good quality photographs of sale items on-line. But, as with film photography, prerequisites such as focus, range, lighting, background and camera shake have an enormous bearing on the end result. So, take the photograph against a neutral background and in natural or controlled lighting (dedicated flash and bounce reflectors being ideal). Make sure that you are within the optimal focusing range of the camera and that, if you are using natural light on a dull day, the camera is steadied by a tripod or at least a beanbag.

Potential purchasers of militaria, especially those of uniform items and cloth regalia, are naturally concerned with the quality of the fabric or material and the strength or, conversely, the fading of colours. Consequently, it is important that photographs accurately reveal the surface condition and colour hues. So make sure that photographs are not taken in the direction of the sun, which has the effect of 'thinning' the colour intensity.

When it comes to uniform items, however, there is no doubt that one of the most important factors required to convince an interested potential purchaser that he should buy your item is to take a good close-up image of the manufacturer's labels. Not only should they clearly reveal the date of manufacture and the pattern number, they will also often betray any interference. Tell-tale evidence of obvious or incongruous stitching often betrays the spurious mismatching of labels, such tampering being designed to make a newer item appear older than it is.

Although sellers do not necessarily need to take up offers of multiple listings, it is worth taking advantage of opportunities to post larger pictures in support of your written description. A good picture, or pictures, supported by an accurate, descriptive text, clearly identifying the manufacturer, date of manufacture, condition and, as honestly as possible, any faults with the item, and you are ready to submit your item for auction.

You should consider what is likely to be the best time to submit your listing. If you are hoping to sell to a British buyer and have opted for the most common, seven-day auction duration, there is really no point in submitting your listing too late at night or mid-morning on a weekday. When the auction closes, many potential bidders will either be asleep or at work. The best time to submit your listing is when most people can find the time to sit unselfishly in front of their PCs. So, midweek after 8.30p.m. when young children are in bed and *EastEnders* has finished is a good time, but Saturday afternoon, when the majority are shopping or at football matches is a bad time, and

Detail of a cheerful Sussex Home Guardsman showing the P17 rifle. A khaki field service cap with Royal Sussex cap badge is worn.

so on.

Pierre Omidyar established Auctionweb, an enthusiasts' on-line trading community, in 1995. His principal motivation was to create an environment where collectors traded with collectors direct. Furthermore, his fiancée Pam, a collector of Pez candy dispensers, wished to meet like-minded enthusiasts; dialogue and the promise of a fair price were the keys and Auctionweb quickly evolved into eBay.

ON-LINE ETIQUETTE

Communities, regardless of commercial intent, depend on co-operation and positive interchange between members. Consequently, when selling on-line it is important to communicate with prospective purchasers, answering their questions and providing additional information should they require it. Although at times rather tedious and frustrating, especially if all the information could have been gleaned from a more thorough reading of your listing description, it pays to be civil and to provide answers. With eBay, for example, famously self-governed by a system of feedback empowering registered users to publish their opinions of a seller's bone fides, it is dangerous to court any potential disapprobation. But, above all, answer questions honestly, a few minutes of emailing supplementary details can save hours of hassle if a purchaser suspects that he is being cheated. In fact, watching how your submission has been received can be quite fascinating; while it is true that, as with traditional auctions bidding takes off at the end, the study of those 'watchers' – potential purchasers who have bookmarked your item ready to come in for the kill shortly before the auction ends – can be quite exciting, and the number of watchers following the progress of your item is also an indication of its popularity.

Once the auction has ended you will discover for how much,

Fatigued, this German army infantry Obergefreiter (corporal) rests his K98 rifle across his lap. He is dressed in early war-period uniform. Note the interior detail of the Stalhelm lining and its chinstrap fixture. Tucked into his belt next to his triple black leather ammunition pouches is his Feldmutz soft head dress and passing over his shoulder are rounds for his section's MG34 machine-gun on a disintegrating link belt. He has a basic black 3rd-class wound badge on his left breast. The letter 'W' on both epaulettes signifies 'garrison battalion Vienna'.

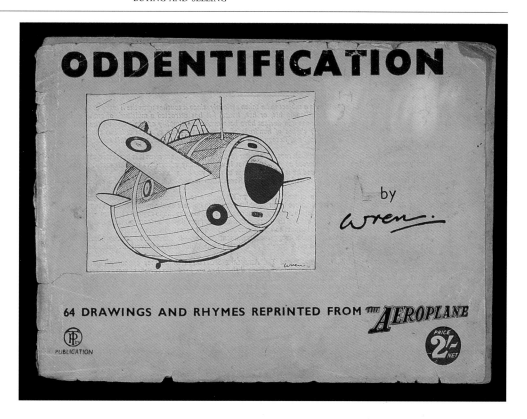

Oddentification. *Cartoons by Wren and accompanying rhymes both reprinted from* The Aeroplane. *Typical of the enormous amount of literature available during wartime in an 'air-minded' Britain.*

or little, you have let your collectable go. Your listing will have specified the payment and postage details, so you will be waiting for either a cheque or confirmation of an electronic bank transfer until you have to package and post your disposed of gem. Avoid any temptation to profit from postage. The authors prefer to specify postal costs clearly, either premium by air or cheaper but much slower by surface mail. However, we carefully pack each item with protective, acid-free, tissue interleafing and the addition of an impregnated paper pest repellent, together with protective bubble wrap or expanded polystyrene packing.

It is perfectly acceptable to charge extra for the time spent packing items carefully and the required consumables. A word of warning about postage rates: it never fails to amaze us how frequently a buyer is prepared to spend hundreds, even thousands of pounds for an item only to quibble over a few pence that he considers excessive.

Buying at on-line auctions is far simpler than selling. It carries none of the obligations a seller can expect. In fact, eBay even offers a function 'Buy It Now' enabling purchasers to circumvent the entire auction process by paying an agreed price up-front. However, opting to sell an item using this facility can be risky since you never know if there is someone out there prepared to pay considerably more than the figure that you thought was most reasonable. Generally, the temptation is to opt for the auction process. Equally, the addition of a reserve can be a

relatively costly option, and especially if the item is unsold; the Buy It Now technique is more suitable for premium items.

Nevertheless, the on-line market place is here to stay. It probably offers the widest ever choice of items for the collector. Registration is simple and, regardless of what some doom merchants may suggest, financial transactions across the internet are mostly secure. Indeed, the majority of credit card providers indemnify cardholders against loss or damage and will refund payment if the purchaser can prove that he never took delivery of the promised goods. And regarding delivery, it is also cheap and easy to insure the value of packages sent overseas. A proof-of-posting receipt gives a unique shipping number and, in Britain, the Royal Mail uses a reliable tracking system enabling the whereabouts and estimated time of arrival of packages to be readily determined.

ON-LINE BONUS
One unexpected benefit of the on-line market place that militaria collectors have discovered is the exchanging of advice and suggestions from interested observers, who, although they may not be in the market for your listed item, offer additional details relating to its provenance. Combined together, all this background information simply adds to our knowledge of historic collectables and it also confirms the real community status of the internet.

12 Values, Trends and Forecasts

As every collector knows, enthusiasts will pay the maximum they can afford if it is for something they really want. A collectable is worth whatever someone is prepared to pay. Beauty is in the eye of the beholder. Individual collections have a value often beyond that of each item. The fact that they have been painstakingly amassed over time and are now arranged either chronologically or in an arm of service classification adds to their value.

Every collector knows that the value of a particular missing item required to complete a set or a series of objects can be way above the market rate. However, we also all know how long we might have to wait for another 'must have' to swim our way and so we are often prepared to pay the premium to save time. Thematic groups are the most valuable; if they are accompanied by evidence of provenance and can be attributed to an individual then their value is further increased.

WHAT DO WE WANT?

Of course, there are certain 'bankers' – items which generally continue to appreciate in investment terms and which always come with a premium price tag. Not surprisingly, as far as twen-

tieth-century militaria are concerned those with the highest value generally emanated from the Third Reich between 1933 and 1945. Authentic items of Nazi uniform or regalia fetch the highest prices in auctions or private sale. First World War artefacts are, like veterans of the Great War, now few and far between. Perishable items of clothing such as tunics, trousers and service caps are much sought after. However, once commonplace items such as webbing and field equipment, now achieve high prices. Authentic First World War helmets, be they of allied or Austro-Hungarian manufacture, also command top prices.

As we have pointed out, original Second World War artefacts are more and more collectable. Premium prices have long been achieved for authentic RAF Battle of Britain-period flying equipment – especially B-type helmets and D-type masks. *Luftwaffe* flying equipment, especially items such as canvas summer-issue flying helmets complete with throat microphones and early issue kapok life preservers are at the top of most enthusiasts' wants lists. The enormous world-wide impact of Hollywood blockbusters such as *Saving Private Ryan* and television series such as *Band of Brothers* have conspired to make once ubiquitous items of

C.1943, armed with a P17 rifle and wearing battledress and field service cap a Sussex Home Guardsman looks out from behind a barricade.

Two Royal Observer Corps members wearing helmets and brassards with civilian clothing. Like other civil defence clothing, this practice predates the adoption of Air Force blue battledress and official blue berets, introduced after 1942. The ROC post is equipped with a Micklethwaite projector, a privately designed device, constructed of items that include Meccano toy wheels; it was used by such volunteers to estimate the height of incoming enemy aircraft.

US Army field equipment highly sought after. Original M1 helmets have always held their value, but, like the equipments of the British and Commonwealth armies, examples of more mundane American webbing and utilitarian service equipment are now highly collectable.

CIVIL DEFENCE

But perhaps the sector that has increased in value the fastest in recent years has been the collecting of home front or civil defence uniforms and equipment. While most collectors were searching for items of Nazi regalia or attempting to complete the field uniform and equipment of wartime Tommies or GIs, it became apparent to others that items from 'Dad's Army' or civil defence forces such as ARP personnel or Germany's *Luftschutz* were worth collecting. Consequently, like an outsider with hitherto unfulfilled potential, home front collectables have quietly raced to the fore in terms of investment value. Now militaria enthusiasts appreciate the significance of wardens' helmets, Home Guard brassards, black-out lamps and ARP first aid kits, and such items are now hard to find. But fortunately, and largely due to the activities of teachers involved in out-reach projects (the British Second World War home front is on the National Curriculum), many hitherto overlooked items have been preserved and, what is more, put to good use in explaining the realities of civilian experience during wartime.

AN UNLOOKED-FOR BONUS

Since the mid 1990s a change in the Ministry of Defence's policy regarding disposals has also been beneficial to collectors of contemporary military clothing. Now unwanted British army uniforms are offered up for sale, especially camouflaged and ceremonial outfits. The previous system saw these items purposely damaged so as to be classified only as rag. This policy was designed for both security reasons and to avoid the possibly disreputable wearing of regimental uniforms, previously worn only for state ceremonial or by the monarch's personal bodyguard. Today, private contractors handle the disposal of unwanted MoD gear instead of by the previous method of disposal via government-run auctions.

This policy change recently presented Sabre Sales with an exciting opportunity. Having purchased thousands of 'sealed patterns' from MoD storage at Didcot, the firm was able to offer collectors some unique items. The 'patterns' are the masters or production prototypes upon which service-issue buttons, badges and military accoutrements are manufactured. This example of bureaucratic rationalization was particularly beneficial to collectors, presenting them with the opportunity to purchase archetypal versions of military items ranging from insignia, clothing and haberdashery, to fixture and fittings spanning the last sixty or so years and covering all three armed services. These fascinating items had been previously unseen by collectors, being sent

ABOVE: Second World War US Army officer's garrison/overseas cap in dark brown ('chocolate') colour. Piped with the black and gold general officer's piping (a system which used coloured piping to identify each branch of service: for example, blue for infantry, red for artillery and yellow for cavalry). Mounted on the left of the cap are the rank bars of a captain. In wartime it was common practice for rank to be worn on this type of headdress, together with being depicted on the uniform shirt or tunic.

LEFT: United Nations peacekeeper's fatigue cap of 1950s vintage. The UN badge sports a French text.

only to the manufacturer tasked with the production of the item specified. A wax seal precisely identified the item's classification, date of introduction and specific use by the army, navy or air force.

THE POWER OF THE INTERNET
Regardless in changes in trends and personal predilections for different types of military collectable, the single biggest development in the hobby is the emergence of the internet - buying and selling online. Principally this means using eBay of course. The power, the 'spread' of eBay delivers a huge, international audience. The extent of this massive PC-empowered marketplace has naturally meant that items are available over a much wider geographical area. For example, North American collectors now readily buy British civil defence items, previously rarely available outside the British Isles. This larger and often more affluent market has reduced the available items and, naturally, pushed up values. The tried and trusted mechanisms of supply and demand have applied premium values to previously mundane items and even the once common British civilian Second World War respirator now has value. In Britain, unlike France the USA there is really no great interest in items from either the Cold War or post- Second World War campaigns such as those in Malaya, Korea, Cyprus, Aden and Borneo. The French, for example, are very interested in items relating to the French Indo-China or Algerian conflicts and Americans snap up items relating to the Vietnam War with relish.

There will always be 'thematic' collectors for the latest editions of service equipment such as helmets and bayonets or items of regalia such as cap badges and medals, and certainly the recent dramatic cull of famous British regiments has encouraged collectors to source once common items. Another area of collecting which continues to thrive is that of post-Second World War awards and medals since they carry their holder's name, as do Great War medals, but those awarded in Britain during the 1939–45 conflict were not and are consequently of less value to collectors; thus, from a research point of view, collectors of British Second World War awards generally search for groups of medals that include a gallantry award or service medal awarded to a named individual.

CAMOUFLAGE
A new theme that has manifested itself since the 1970s is the collecting of world camouflage. This is an ever evolving field because there is so much available and so many variations to collect. These variations of camouflage patterns occur not just in regular but also increasingly in special forces, the cache attached to combat gear worn by elite forces is considerable. The numerous small, almost private armies involved in African, Middle Eastern and Far Eastern conflicts, each garbed in a wide variety of bespoke designs, has added to the choice available.

But if a collector simply opts for American camouflage there is a huge variety of examples to choose from. Popular choices include the US Army/Marine Corps camouflage developed during the Second World War, later colloquially known as 'duck hunter', and progressing via the use of the American special forces 'tiger stripe' camos developed during the Vietnam War through to the Marine Corps' early 1970s' 'erdel' pattern (the familiar design featured on 'Nam-period helmet covers).

However, there is a lot more. The US Army universally adopted the 'Woodland' camouflage pattern from the mid to the late 1970s, a pattern that was extensively copied by armies in Latin America, South-East Asia and, more recently, by European armies in the Balkans. Furthermore, conflicts in Somalia and the Gulf have added to the variety. Perhaps the most famous of these, popularized on television during the first Gulf War, was the classic 'chocolate chip' pattern (also known as 'cookie dough'). This six-colour camouflage of tans, browns, black and white was intended to simulate a stone-strewn desert terrain. Interestingly, it was developed as long ago as the 1960s as part of an American contingency plan to prepare for possible involvement in future Arab-Israeli conflicts. However, once in theatre, American armies discovered that they were clothed too similarly to their Arab allies, many of whom they had, of course, originally equipped. Keen to differentiate their forces from others and after discovering that,

ABOVE: *Third Reich pin badges and insignia. From left to right: police arm patch for Berlin; selection of rally badges and party organization pins (including party membership badge,* NSKK, Hitler Youth, BDM, Winterhilfe, *Deutsches* Red Cross, Frauenshaft *and a variety of sports organizations. In the box is a twenty-five-year service medal.*

RIGHT: *A member of the LDV in late summer 1940. The soldier is wearing the army's early pattern denim battledress (all that could be spared for such volunteer troops after the devastating loss of almost all the BEF's clothing stocks in France). His ammunition is carried in a cotton bandolier of American origin like his P17 rifle. A civil respirator is still carried, however, as military pattern ones had yet to be issued to such irregulars.*

ABOVE: *1940's vintage, British Red Cross women's' uniform cap worn with thecorresponding blue service dress uniform. The ribbon band is in the collars of the organisation. The design is effectively that of an early A.T.S. cap. British Red Cross uniform was manufactured privately for the organisation not strictly coming under the control of the British government.*

Selection of British Second World War home defence equipment arranged against a rare Home Guard Flag. Belonging to 8th Battalion City of London Home Guard the flag was one of eight presented to battalions of 'J' Zone Home Guard on June 11th 1944 (8 and 35 City of London Btts. And 51,52,53,54,55 and 56 Essex Btts). Other items shown include Home Guard uniforms and brassards, FS cap, entrenching tool handles converted to accept the bayonet for the new NO 4 rifle and a 'Swift Target Rifle'. This weapon, a training aid, fired a pin into a paper target mounted at the end of the barrel. The pin pricks displayed accuracy of fire.

in fact, the design did not actually blend in with the terrain too well, and being so elaborate that it cost a fortune to print, the USA soon adopted another scheme. The new design presented a more random pattern of desert camouflage and was cheaper, being of only three colours. However, no sooner was this pattern established than it was in its turn superseded. The most recent American camouflage designs are very twentieth-first-century. Based on micro patterns of digitally-produced pixels and developed and, furthermore, patented by the US Marine Corps, 'Marpat' (MARine Disruptive PATtern) is available in two colour schemes: woodland and desert. An urban pattern was also designed but never officially adopted.

Because of the current 'War on Terrorism', recent security concerns in the USA have imposed much tighter controls on the sale and disposal of surplus military uniforms. This means that far fewer examples are available to collectors and enthusiasts. It should be borne in mind, however, that in North America so much official military style has been copied and adopted by both the outdoor community and the fashionistas that a wide variety of similar designs are available commercially.

THE FUTURE

Finally, there is no doubt that, given the paucity of new material available, and by 'new' we mean previously unavailable items of twentieth-century militaria, for it to continue the trade in such collectables will depend on the redistribution of what already exists. The internet will be an essential part of this process, as it already is in facilitating the activities of on-line dealers and auction houses. However, it is assumed that there will be a growing trend in the development of on-line communities of militaria collectors seeking either a missing collar badge or perhaps the definition of an obscure Austro-Hungarian button dating from the Great War. It is therefore possible that, for once, the enthusiast rather than the dealer will play the larger part in the survival of the hobby as more items and advice are swapped and proffered without an accompanying desire for commercial gain. This development could see an evolution of the hobby as radical as that which has taken place in less than a decade with the disappearance of many high street outlets and the hegemony of the internet as the new medium of exchange – in every sense.

Index